CAPRICORN
2000

GW00482758

With love to Bill, Jean, Rob and Shani

This is the third year that I've written these books and it's about time I thanked all the people who help me to put them together. I have worked with some of them since the beginning of the books, and others have only recently started lending me their help, but I am immensely grateful to them all. So thank you, Nova Jayne Heath, Nicola Chalton, Nick Robinson and everyone else at Robinson Publishing for being such a great team to work with. Thanks to Chelsey Fox for all her agenting skills. And a huge thank you to Annie Lionnet and Jamie Macphail for their tireless work.

CAPRICORN
2000

Jane Struthers

First published in 1999 by Parragon

Parragon
Queen Street House
4 Queen Street
Bath BA1 1HE
UK

Produced by Magpie Books, an imprint of
Robinson Publishing Ltd, London

Illustrations courtesy of Slatter-Anderson, London

ISBN 0 75252 899 8

A copy of the British Library Cataloguing-in-Publication Data
is available from the British Library

Printed and bound in the EC

CONTENTS

Dates for 2000

Capricorn 21 December – 19 January

Aquarius 20 January – 18 February

Pisces 19 February – 19 March

Aries 20 March – 18 April

Taurus 19 April – 19 May

Gemini 20 May – 20 June

Cancer 21 June – 21 July

Leo 22 July – 21 August

Virgo 22 August – 21 September

Libra 22 September – 22 October

Scorpio 23 October – 21 November

Sagittarius 22 November – 20 December

YOUR CAPRICORN SUN SIGN

This chapter is all about your Sun sign. I'm going to describe your general personality, as well as the way you react in relationships, how you handle money, what your health is like and which careers suit you. But before I do all that, I want to explain what a Sun sign is. It's the sign that the Sun occupied at the time of your birth. Every year, the Sun moves through the sky, spending an average of 30 days in each of the signs. You're a Capricorn, which means that you were born when the Sun was moving through the sign of Capricorn. It's the same as saying that Capricorn is your star sign, but astrologers prefer to use the term 'Sun sign' because it's more accurate.

Character

It can be tough being a Capricorn. The moment they hear what your Sun sign is, people tend to misunderstand you and to write you off as a bit boring. 'Gosh, a Capricorn', they smile uneasily. 'How, er, interesting.'

Well, it's about time that Capricorns were given the praise they deserve. Yes, you can be guilty of bleak pessimism and you can become horribly depressed sometimes but you're very dependable and you've got a fantastic sense of humour – often directed at yourself. In fact, your wonderful humour is frequently your saving grace – not only does it help you to put problems in perspective but anyone who's enjoyed a good laugh with you will always want to come back for more. Who wouldn't?

Another of your greatest strengths is the ability to learn from experience. Some signs keep making the same errors over and over again, but it's an unusual Capricorn who can't turn a bad mistake into a valuable lesson sooner or later. You may not agree, of course – you can suffer from a lack of confidence that makes you doubt your own abilities and feel inferior to others, even when this isn't justified.

While the rest of the zodiac age as they get older, that process seems to work in reverse for Capricorns. Very often you begin life with an old head on young shoulders, making you act much older than your years would suggest. Yet, as you grow older, the normal ageing process goes into reverse and you somehow become younger. You mellow, learn to relax and can be quite skittish by middle-age.

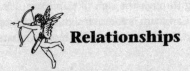# Relationships

You may seem calm and collected on the surface, but you're not nearly as emotionally unruffled as you appear. Deep down, you're extremely shy and vulnerable. Your feelings are easily hurt, even if you don't let on, and over the years you may learn to distance yourself emotionally from people as a form of protection. Yet that doesn't stop you feeling things deeply, even if you can't bring yourself to show it. In fact, Capricorns aren't noted for their demonstrative affections, and you can feel quite constrained about letting people know how you feel. What happens if you're rebuffed or rejected? you wonder. How will you cope? So you try to avoid emotional scenes and you may even shy away from close relationships altogether, so you don't run the risk of being hurt. Unfortunately, this attitude can cause difficulties with loved ones, who misinterpret your reserve and think it's indifference. Make sure they know that you care for them.

 **Money**

You have a healthy respect for money and what it can buy. It's no coincidence that there are many jokes about the Capricorn streak of meanness. You certainly don't like to fritter money away, although once you're well-heeled you can be surprisingly open-handed when buying major purchases. Mind you, you'll still be reluctant to part with small amounts of cash – the person who drives from one supermarket to the next in the quest for the cheapest prices is usually a Capricorn.

Money also means a lot because it offers you material and emotional security. These are both essential ingredients of your happiness. You'll be reluctant to get married or start a family until you know you can afford to do so – you hate the thought of a hand-to-mouth existence and will work round the clock to ensure you earn enough money to live comfortably.

When investing that hard-earned cash, you like to buy things that will last a long time. Fads and fashions pass you by – what you're looking for is durability and quality. You have a natural affinity with big business so may become interested in dabbling on the stock market, but only if you're certain there's little risk of losing your shirt.

Health

Stop worrying! You're one of the signs noted for your ability to fret and feel anxious, partly because you have such a strong sense of responsibility, thanks to your strict ruler, Saturn. Learning to relax properly has a dramatic impact on your energy levels, and will also improve your sleeping patterns. If you can't unwind by yourself, get involved in a hobby that allows you to keep active while engaging your mind – gardening suits you well, because contact with the ground complements your Earth element and you benefit from being in the fresh air.

The body's skeletal structure is ruled by Capricorn, so you need to take care of your bones in general and your knees in particular. Try to live in a warm, dry atmosphere because you're very vulnerable to the cold and damp. Unfortunately you can be susceptible to arthritis, so you should get plenty of gentle exercise to prevent becoming stiff and seizing up. You can also have problems with your teeth – could that explain the sinking feeling that comes over you whenever you pass a dentist's surgery?

Career

This is one area of life that you usually feel very confident about. You consider your career to be a way of proving yourself, and you may devote a lot of time to it. Yet you may have several false starts or feel that you aren't getting very far at first. That's because life is often a struggle for Capricorns until they reach their thirtieth birthdays, after which things become much easier and their careers begin to take off. Whatever your age, your job is very important to you because you need to prove that you're a success and can make your own way through life. You're extremely ambitious, and may have secret plans about heading straight for the top of your particular tree. What's more, you stand an excellent chance of succeeding, no matter how long it takes.

You're an invaluable member of a team, thanks to your diligence, pragmatism and patience. Bosses and colleagues know they can rely on you to get things done – you won't let them down. This strong sense of duty can keep you chained to your desk long after everyone else has gone home, and can turn you into a workaholic (with your family complaining that they never see you), but you can't imagine behaving in any other way.

Among the professions that are ideally suited to you are big business, dentistry, the civil service and government work. You cope well with responsible jobs, and even if it is lonely at the top you'll be able to manage beautifully.

MERCURY AND YOUR COMMUNICATIONS

Where would we be without Mercury? This tiny planet rules everything connected with our communications, from the way we speak to the way we get about. The position of Mercury in your birth chart describes how fast or how slow you absorb information, the sorts of things you talk about, the way you communicate with other people and how much nervous energy you have.

Mercury is an important part of everyone's birth chart, but it has extra meaning for Geminis and Virgos because both these signs are ruled by Mercury.

Mercury is the closest planet to the Sun in the solar system, and its orbit lies between the Earth and the Sun. In fact, it is never more than 28 degrees away from the Sun. Mercury is one of the smallest known planets in the solar system, but it makes up in speed what it lacks in size. It whizzes around the Sun at about 108,000 miles an hour, to avoid being sucked into the Sun's fiery mass.

If you've always wondered how astrology works, here's a brief explanation. Your horoscope (a map of the planets' positions at the time of your birth) is divided up into twelve sections, known as 'houses'. Each one represents a different area of your life, and together they cover every aspect of our experiences on Earth. As Mercury moves around the heavens each year it progresses through each house in turn, affecting a particular part of your life, such as your health or career. If you plot its progress through your own chart, you'll be able to make the most of Mercury's influence in 2000. That way, you'll know when it's best to make contact with others and when it's wisest to keep your thoughts to yourself.

Mercury takes just over one year to complete its orbit of the Earth, but during this time it doesn't always travel forwards, it also appears to go backwards. When this happens, it means that, from our vantage point on Earth, Mercury has slowed down to such an extent that it seems to be backtracking through the skies. We call this retrograde motion. When Mercury is travelling forwards, we call it direct motion.

All the planets, with the exception of the Sun and Moon, go retrograde at some point during their orbit of the Earth. A retrograde Mercury is very important because it means that during this time our communications can hit delays and snags. Messages may go missing, letters could get lost in the post, appliances and gadgets can go on the blink. You may also find it hard to make yourself understood. In 2000, there are several periods when Mercury goes retrograde. These are between 21 February and 14 March, 23 June and 17 July, and between 18 October and 8 November. These are all times to keep a close eye on your communications. You may also feel happiest if you can avoid signing important agreements or contracts during these times.

To plot the progress of Mercury, fill in the blank diagram on page 8, writing '1' in the section next to your Sun sign, then numbering consecutively in an anti-clockwise direction around the signs until you have completed them all. It will now be easy to chart Mercury's movements. When it is in the same sign as your Sun, Mercury is in your first house, when he moves into the next sign (assuming he's not going retrograde) he occupies your second house, and so on, until he reaches your twelfth house, at which point he will move back into your first house again.

Diagram 1

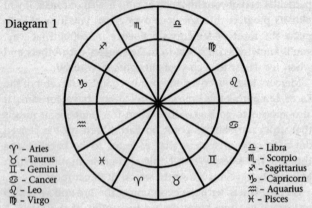

♈ – Aries
♉ – Taurus
♊ – Gemini
♋ – Cancer
♌ – Leo
♍ – Virgo

♎ – Libra
♏ – Scorpio
♐ – Sagittarius
♑ – Capricorn
♒ – Aquarius
♓ – Pisces

Here are the houses of the horoscope, numbered from one to twelve, for someone born with the Sun in Aquarius.

Diagram 2

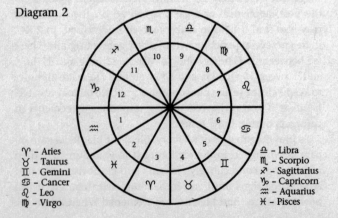

♈ – Aries
♉ – Taurus
♊ – Gemini
♋ – Cancer
♌ – Leo
♍ – Virgo

♎ – Libra
♏ – Scorpio
♐ – Sagittarius
♑ – Capricorn
♒ – Aquarius
♓ – Pisces

MERCURY'S ENTRY INTO THE SIGNS IN 2000
(All times are given in GMT, using the 24-hour clock)

January
Mercury is in Capricorn when 2000 begins

18	22:21	Aquarius

February

5	08:10	Pisces
21	12:47	Retrograde in Pisces

March

14	20:40	Direct in Pisces

April

13	00:18	Aries
30	03:54	Taurus

May

14	07:11	Gemini
30	04:28	Cancer

June

23	08:33	Retrograde in Cancer

July

17	13:21	Direct in Cancer

August

7	05:43	Leo
22	10:12	Virgo

September

7	21:23	Libra
28	13:29	Scorpio

October

18	13:42	Retrograde in Scorpio

November		
7	07:29	Retrograde into Libra
8	02:29	Direct in Libra
8	21:43	Scorpio

December		
3	20:27	Sagittarius
23	02:04	Capricorn

As 2000 begins, Mercury is moving through the final degrees of Capricorn, so it is in whichever house corresponds with the sign of Capricorn in your diagram. For instance, if you're an Aquarian, Mercury will move into your own sign at 22:21 GMT on 18 January and will occupy your first house. You can then read the explanation below telling you what to expect at this time. Mercury next moves signs at 08:10 GMT on 5 February, when he moves into Pisces. So if you're an Aquarian, Mercury will now be in your second house.

Mercury in the First House

This is a very busy time for you and you're completely wrapped up in your own ideas and concerns. Even if you aren't usually very chatty, you certainly are at the moment. However, you will much prefer talking about yourself to listening to other people! You've got lots of nervous energy at the moment and you'll enjoy getting out and about as much as possible. Look for ways of burning off excess energy, such as going for brisk walks or doing things that require initiative. This is a great opportunity to think about ways of pushing forward with ideas and getting new projects off the ground.

Mercury in the Second House

This is a great time to think about things that mean a lot to you. These might be beliefs, philosophies or anything else that gives meaning to your life. It's also a good time to consider the people that make your world go round. Do you devote enough time to them? You should also spare a thought for your finances, because this is a perfect opportunity to scrutinize them and make sure everything is in order. You could get in touch with someone who can give you some financial advice, or you might do some research into how to put your money to good use.

Mercury in the Third House

Chatty? You bet! This is probably when you're at your most talkative, and you'll enjoy nattering away about whatever pops into your head. You'll love talking to whoever happens to be around, but you'll get on especially well with neighbours, people you see in the course of your daily routine and close relatives. You'll soon start to feel restless if you have to spend too long in one place, so grab every opportunity to vary your schedule. You'll love taking off on day trips, going away for weekend breaks or simply abandoning your usual routine and doing something completely different. Communications will go well and you'll love playing with gadgets and appliances.

Mercury in the Fourth House

Your thoughts are never far away from your home and family life at the moment. You may be thinking about ways of improving your living standards and you could talk to people who can give you some advice. You're also wrapped up in thoughts of the past, and you may even be assailed by memories of far-off events or things you haven't thought about in ages. Pay attention to your dreams because they could give you some invaluable insights into the way you're feeling. Watch out for a slight tendency to be defensive or to imagine that people are trying to get at you. It's a lovely time for getting in touch with your nearest and dearest who live a long way away.

Mercury in the Fifth House

You'll really enjoy putting your mind to good use at the moment, especially if you do things that are based on fun. For instance, you might get engrossed in competitions, jigsaw puzzles, crosswords and quizzes, especially if there's the chance of winning a prize! Children and pets will be terrific company and you'll love romping with them. However, you may find that they're a lot more playful than usual. You may even be on the receiving end of some practical jokes. It's a super time to go on holiday, particularly if you're visiting somewhere you've never been before. Your social life promises to keep you busy and you'll find it easy to talk to loved ones about things that matter to you.

Mercury in the Sixth House

This is the ideal time of year to think about your health and well-being. Are you looking after yourself properly? If you've been battling with some strange symptoms, this is the perfect opportunity to get them investigated so you can put your mind at rest. You'll enjoy reading about medical matters, such as immersing yourself in a book that tells you how to keep fit or extolling the virtues of a specific eating plan. Your work might also keep you busy. Colleagues and customers will be chatty, and you could spend a lot of time dealing with paperwork or tapping away on the computer. It's a great time to look for a new job, especially if that means scanning the newspaper adverts, joining an employment agency or writing lots of application letters.

Mercury in the Seventh House

Communications play an important role in all your relationships at the moment. This is your chance to put across your point of view and to keep other people posted about what you think. You may enjoy having lots of chats with partners or you might have something important to discuss. Either way, the key to success is to keep talking! You're prepared to reach a compromise, so it's a marvellous time to get involved in negotiations and discussions. You'll also find that two heads are better than one right now, so it's the ideal time to do some teamwork. You'll enjoy bouncing your ideas off other people and listening to what they have to say.

Mercury in the Eighth House

It's time to turn your attention to your shared resources and official money matters. So if you share a bank account with your partner, you should check that everything is running smoothly. You might even decide to open a new account that suits you better or that pays a higher rate of interest. Speaking of accounts, this is an excellent time to fill in your tax return or complete your accounts for the year because you're in the right frame of mind for such things. This is also a good time to think about your close relationships. Do they bring you the emotional satisfaction that you need or is something missing? If you think there's room for improvement, talk to your partner about how to make things better between you.

Mercury in the Ninth House

The more you can expand your mental and physical horizons now, the happier you'll be. It's a time of year when you're filled with intellectual curiosity about the world and you long to cram your head with all sorts of facts and figures. You might decide to do some studying, whether you do it on a very informal basis or enrol for an evening class or college course. You'll certainly enjoy browsing around bookshops and library shelves, looking for books on your favourite subjects. Travel will appeal to you too, especially if you can visit somewhere exotic or a place that you've never been to before. You might become interested in a different religion from your own or you could be engrossed in something connected with philosophy, history or spirituality.

Mercury in the Tenth House

Spend some time thinking about your career prospects. Are you happy with the way things are going or does your professional life need a rethink? This is a great opportunity to talk to people who can give you some good advice. It's also an excellent time to share your ideas with your boss or a superior, especially if you're hoping to impress them. You could hear about a promotion or some improved job prospects, or you might decide to apply for a completely new job. It's also a marvellous opportunity to increase your qualifications, perhaps by training for something new or brushing up on an existing skill. You'll find it easier than usual to talk to older friends and relatives, especially if they can sometimes be a little tricky or hard to please.

Mercury in the Eleventh House

This is a great time to enjoy the company of friends and acquaintances. You'll love talking to them, especially if you can chat about subjects that make you think or that have humanitarian overtones. All sorts of intellectual activities will appeal to you at the moment. If your social circle is getting smaller and smaller, grab this chance to widen your horizons by meeting people who are on the same wavelength as you. For instance, you might decide to join a new club or society that caters for one of your interests. It's also a good opportunity to think about your hopes and wishes for the future. Are they going according to plan, or should you revise your strategy or even start again from scratch?

Mercury in the Twelfth House

You're entering a very reflective and reclusive period when you want to retreat from the madding crowd and have some time to yourself. You might enjoy taking the phone off the hook and curling up with a good book, or you could spend time studying subjects by yourself. There will be times when you feel quite tongue-tied, and you'll find it difficult to say exactly what you mean. You may even want to maintain a discreet silence on certain subjects, but make sure that other people don't take advantage of this by putting words into your mouth. You could be the recipient of someone's confidences, in which case you'll be a sympathetic listener. If you want to tell someone your secrets, choose your confidante wisely.

LOVE AND THE STARS

Love makes the world go round. When we know we're loved, we walk on air. We feel confident, happy and joyous. Without love, we feel miserable, lonely and as if life isn't worth living. If you're still looking for your perfect partner, this is the ideal guide for you. It will tell you which Sun signs you get on best with and which ones aren't such easy-going mates. By the way, there is hope for every astrological combination, and none are out and out disasters. It's simply that you'll find it easier to get on well with some signs than with others.

At the end of this section you'll see two compatibility charts – one showing how you get on in the love and sex stakes, and the other one telling you which signs make the best friends. These charts will instantly remind you which signs get on best and which struggle to keep the peace. Each combination has been given marks out of ten, with ten points being a fabulous pairing and one point being pretty grim. Find the woman's Sun sign along the top line of the chart, then look down the left-hand column for the man's sign. The square where these two lines meet will give you the result of this astrological combination. For instance, when assessing the love and sex compatibility of a Leo woman and a Cancerian man, they score six out of ten.

Capricorn

Despite their outward poise, a Capricorn is very easily hurt so
they need to know their feelings won't be trampled on.
There's least danger of that when they get together with a
fellow Earth sign. A Capricorn adores a Taurean's deep sense of
responsibility and they'll both work hard to create their ideal
home. A Capricorn appreciates the methodical approach of a
Virgo, but could feel deeply hurt by the Virgo's sharp tongue
and caustic remarks. If two Capricorns team up, one of them
must be demonstrative and openly affectionate, otherwise the
relationship could be rather sterile and serious.

Capricorns also feel safe with members of the Water signs.
When a Capricorn gets together with a Cancerian, they do
their utmost to make their home a haven. They'll get great
satisfaction from channelling their energies into bringing up a
family. A Capricorn may be rather bemused by the depth and
intensity of a Scorpio's emotions – Capricorns are too reserved
to indulge in such drama themselves and it can make them
feel uncomfortable. A no-nonsense Capricorn could be perplexed by an extremely vulnerable Piscean and won't know
how to handle them. Should they give them a hanky or tell
them to pull themselves together?

The Air signs can also make a Capricorn feel somewhat
unsettled. They're fascinated by a Gemini's breadth of
knowledge and endless chat, but they also find them superficial and rather flighty. In fact, the Capricorn probably
doesn't trust the Gemini. A Capricorn feels far happier in
the company of a Libran. Here's someone who seems much
steadier emotionally and who can help the Capricorn to
unwind after a hard day's work. It can be great or ghastly
when a Capricorn sets their sights on an Aquarian. They
understand each other provided the Aquarian isn't too
unconventional, but the Capricorn feels uncomfortable

and embarrassed by any displays of eccentricity, deliberate or not.

The Fire signs help to warm up the Capricorn, who can be rather remote and distant at times. A Capricorn admires the Arien's drive and initiative, but endlessly tells them to look before they leap and could become irritated when they don't take this sage advice. When a Capricorn gets together with a Leo, they won't need to worry about appearances – the Capricorn will feel justly proud of the smart Leo. However, they could wince when the bills come in and they discover how much those clothes cost. A Capricorn thinks a Sagittarian must have come from another planet – how can they be so relaxed and laid-back all the time? They have great respect for the Sagittarian's wisdom and philosophy, but they quickly become fed up with having to fit in around the Sagittarian's hectic social life.

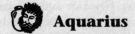

Aquarius

Put an Aquarian with a fellow Air sign and they're happy. They thoroughly enjoy being with a lively Gemini and love discussing everything under the sun with them. They may not have a very exciting sex life, but their mental closeness will more than make up for it. The gentle charms of a Libran calms down an Aquarian when their nerves become frayed, although they disapprove of the Libran's innate tact and diplomacy – why can't they just say what they think, instead of sitting on the fence? With two Aquarians you never know what to expect, other than that they'll be great friends. They'll certainly do a lot of talking, but could spend more time debating esoteric ideas and abstract concepts.

An Aquarian likes all the Fire signs, although they find

Ariens hard to fathom and can become exhausted by an Arien's endless supply of energy and enthusiasm. There are no such problems when an Aquarian pairs up with a Leo because they complement each other in many ways. The Aquarian teaches objectivity to the Leo, who in return encourages the Aquarian to express their emotions more. An Aquarian thoroughly enjoys being with a Sagittarian because both of them hate being tied down. As a result, they respect one another's independence and will probably rarely see each other because of all their spare-time activities.

It's not quite so simple when an Aquarian joins forces with one of the Earth signs. An Aquarian will lock horns with a Taurean sooner or later, because neither of them is able to back down once a disagreement has started. The Aquarian will also feel very restricted by the Taurean's possessiveness. The Virgo's analytical approach to life intrigues the Aquarian but they'll sit up all night arguing the toss over everything, with each one convinced that they've got all the answers. When an Aquarian meets a Capricorn, they've got their work cut out for them if they're to find a happy medium between the erratic Aquarian and the conventional Capricorn.

An Aquarian feels out of their depth when they're with one of the Water signs. They simply don't understand what makes a Cancerian tick – why do they worry themselves sick over things that they can't change? The Aquarian finds it all most peculiar. They also find it difficult to understand a Scorpio who takes so many things so seriously. Although the Aquarian also has a list of topics that mean a lot to them, they're not the sort of things that hold the slightest interest for a Scorpio. It's more or less the same story with a Pisces, because their huge resources of emotion make the Aquarian feel uncomfortable and fill them with a strong desire to escape as fast as possible.

 Pisces

Relationships mean a lot to a sensitive Piscean, but they're easily misunderstood by many of the more robust signs. There are no such worries with the other Water signs, however. A Piscean loves being with a tender Cancerian who knows how to help them relax and feel safe. They really enjoy playing house together but the emotional scenes will blow the roof off. The relationship between a Piscean and a Scorpio can be quite spicy and sexy, but the Piscean is turned off if the Scorpio becomes too intense and dramatic. Two Pisceans feel safe with one another, but they'll push all their problems under the carpet unless one of them is more objective.

A Piscean also gets on well with the Earth signs, although with a few reservations. A Piscean takes comfort from being looked after by a protective Taurean, but after a while they could feel stifled by the Taurean's possessive and matter-of-fact attitude. The relationship between a Piscean and a Virgo starts off well but the Piscean could soon feel crushed by the Virgo's criticism and will need more emotional reassurance than the Virgo is able to give. A Piscean feels safe with a Capricorn because they're so dependable but in the end this may begin to bug them. It's not that they want the Capricorn to two-time them, more that they'd like a little unpredictability every now and then.

A Piscean is fascinated by the Air signs but their apparent lack of emotion could cause problems. A Piscean and a Gemini are terrific friends but could encounter difficulties as lovers. The Piscean's strong emotional needs are too much for the Gemini to handle – they'll feel as if they're drowning. The Piscean is on much firmer ground with a Libran, who'll go out of their way to keep the Piscean happy. Neither sign is good at facing up to any nasty truths, however. An Aquarian is too much for a sensitive Piscean, who views the world through rose-coloured specs. An Aquarian, on the other hand, has uncomfortably clear vision.

The Fire signs can cheer up a Piscean enormously, but any prolonged displays of emotion will make the Fire signs feel weighed down. The Piscean is fascinated by an Arien's exploits but could feel reluctant to join in. They'll also be easily hurt by some of the Arien's off-the-cuff remarks. When a Piscean pairs up with a Leo they appreciate the way the Leo wants to take charge and look after them. After a while, however, this could grate on them and they'll want to be more independent. A Piscean enjoys discussing philosophy and spiritual ideas with a Sagittarian – they can sit up half the night talking things through. The Sagittarian brand of honesty could hurt the Piscean at times, but they know this isn't malicious and will quickly forgive such outbursts.

🐏 Aries

Because Ariens belong to the Fire element, they get on very well with their fellow Fire signs Leo and Sagittarius. All the same, an Arien getting together with a Leo will soon notice a distinct drop in their bank balance, because they'll enjoy going to all the swankiest restaurants and sitting in the best seats at the theatre. When an Arien pairs up with a Sagittarian, they'll compete over who drives the fastest car and has the most exciting holidays. When two Ariens get together the results can be combustible. Ideally, one Arien should be a lot quieter, otherwise they'll spend most of their time jostling for power. All these combinations are very sexy and physical.

Ariens also thrive in the company of the three Air signs – Gemini, Libra and Aquarius. Of the three, they get on best with Geminis, who share their rather childlike view of the world and also their sense of fun. An Arien and a Gemini enjoy hatching all sorts of ideas and schemes, even if they never get round to putting them into action. There's an exciting sense of friction between Aries and Libra, their opposite number in the zodiac. An Arien will be enchanted by the way their Libran caters to their every need, but may become impatient when the Libran also wants to look after other people. An Arien will be captivated by the originality of an Aquarian, although at times they'll be driven mad by the Aquarian's eccentric approach to life and the way they blow hot and cold in the bedroom.

Ariens don't do so well with the Earth signs – Taurus, Virgo and Capricorn. The very careful, slightly plodding nature of a typical Taurean can drive an Arien barmy at times, and although they'll respect – and benefit from – the Taurean's practical approach to life, it can still fill them with irritation. An Arien finds it difficult to fathom a Virgo, because their attitudes to life are diametrically opposed. An Arien likes to jump in with both feet, while a Virgo prefers to take things slowly and analyse every possibility before committing themselves. An Arien can get on quite well with a Capricorn, because they're linked by their sense of ambition and their earthy sexual needs.

An Arien is out of their depth with any of the Water signs – Cancer, Scorpio and Pisces. They quickly become irritated by the defensive Cancerian, although they'll love their cooking. An Arien will enjoy a very passionate affair with a Scorpio, but the Scorpio's need to know exactly what the Arien is up to when their back is turned will soon cause problems and rifts. Although an Arien may begin a relationship with a Pisces by wanting to look after them and protect them from the harsh realities of life, eventually the Piscean's extremely sensitive nature may bring out the Arien's bullying streak.

🐂 Taurus

Taureans are literally in their element when they're with Virgos or Capricorns who, like themselves, are Earth signs. Two Taureans will get along very happily together, although they could become so wedded to routine that they get stuck in a rut. They may also encourage one another to eat too much. A Taurean will enjoy being with a Virgo, because they respect the Virgo's methodical nature. They'll also like encouraging their Virgo to relax and take life easy. Money will form a link between a Taurean and a Capricorn, with plenty of serious discussions on how to make it and what to do with it once they've got it. There will also be a strong sexual rapport, and the Taurean will encourage the more sensual side of the Capricorn.

The relationship between a Taurean and members of the Water element is also very good. A Taurean and a Cancerian will revel in one another's company and will probably be so happy at home that they'll rarely stir from their armchairs. They both have a strong need for emotional security and will stick together through thick and thin. There's plenty of passion when a Taurean pairs up with a Scorpio, although the faithful Taurean could become fed up with the Scorpio's jealous nature. They simply won't understand what they're being accused of, and their loyal nature will be offended by the very thought that they could be a two-timer. A Taurean will be delighted by a delicate Piscean, and will want to take care of such a vulnerable and sensitive creature.

Things become rather more complicated when a Taurean pairs up with an Arien, Leo or Sagittarian, all of whom are Fire signs. They have very little in common – Taureans like to take things slowly while Fire signs want to make things happen *now*. It's particularly difficult between a Taurean and an Arien – the careful Taurean will feel harried and rushed by the impetuous Arien. It's a little better when a Taurean gets together with a Leo, because they share a deep appreciation of the good things in life, although the Taurean will be horrified by the Leo's ability to spend money. Making joint decisions could be difficult, however, because they'll both stand their ground and refuse to budge. A Taurean and a Sagittarian simply don't understand each other – they're on such different wavelengths. Any Taurean displays of possessiveness will make the independent Sagittarian want to run a mile.

Taureans are equally mystified by the Air signs – Gemini, Libra and Aquarius. What they see as the flightiness of Gemini drives them barmy – why can't the Gemini settle down and do one thing at a time? The Taurean will probably feel quite exhausted by the Gemini's many interests and bubbly character. Taurus and Libra are a surprisingly good pairing, because they share a need for beauty, luxury and love. This could end up costing the penny-wise Taurean quite a packet, but they'll have a deliciously romantic time along the way. Taurus and Aquarius are chalk and cheese, and neither one is prepared to meet the other one halfway. The Taurean need to keep tabs on their loved one's every movement will irritate the freedom-loving Aquarian, and there will be plenty of rows as a result.

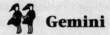

Gemini

One of the Air signs, Geminis get on very well with their fellow members of this element – Librans and Aquarians. Two Geminis are the astrological equivalent of double trouble – they chat nineteen to the dozen and revel in the company of someone who understands them so well. A Gemini delights in being with a Libran, because they enjoy the intellectual company and will benefit from the Libran's (usually) relaxed approach to life. They'll also learn to deal with their emotions more if a sympathetic Libran can guide them. Gemini and Aquarius is a very exciting pairing – the Gemini is encouraged to think deeply and knows that the Aquarian won't put up with any woolly ideas or fudged arguments.

Geminis also get on well with the three Fire signs – Aries, Leo and Sagittarius. A Gemini loves being with a racy, adventurous Arien, and together they enjoy keeping abreast of all the latest gossip and cultural developments. However, after the first flush of enthusiasm has worn off, the Gemini may find the Arien's strong need for sex rather hard to take. The Gemini gets on very well with a Leo. They delight in the Leo's affectionate nature and are amused by their need to have the best that money can buy – and they'll gladly share in the spoils. Gemini and Sagittarius are an excellent combination, because they sit opposite each other in the zodiac and so complement one another's character. The Gemini will be fascinated by the erudite and knowledgeable Sagittarian.

Gemini doesn't do so well with the Earth signs of Taurus and Capricorn, although they get on better with Virgo. The Gemini finds it difficult to understand a Taurean, because they see the world from such different viewpoints. The Gemini takes a more light-hearted approach and lives life at such a speed that they find it difficult to slow down to the more measured pace of a Taurean. The wonderfully dry Capricorn sense of humour is a source of constant delight to a Gemini. However, they're less taken with the Capricorn's streak of pessimism and their love of tradition. Of the three Earth signs, Gemini and Virgo are the most compatible. The Gemini shares the Virgo's brainpower and they have long, fascinating conversations.

When a Gemini gets together with the Water signs, the result can be enjoyable or puzzling. Gemini and Cancer have little in common, because the Gemini wants to spread their emotional and intellectual wings, whereas a Cancerian likes to stay close to home and has little interest in abstract ideas. Gemini finds

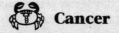

Scorpio perplexing because they operate on such different levels. A Gemini tends to skim along the surface of things, so often deals with life on a superficial level, whereas a Scorpio likes to dig deep and has to have an emotional investment in everything they do. A Gemini appreciates the subtlety and sensitivity of a Piscean, but they're likely to make off-the-cuff comments that unwittingly hurt the Piscean.

Cancer

Cancerians revel in the company of their fellow Water signs of Scorpio and Pisces. When two Cancerians get together they could spend most of their time at home or eating – preferably both. They feel safe in the knowledge that they both have a strong need for love, but their innate Cancerian tenacity may mean they cling on to the relationship even if it's long past its best. A Cancerian is enchanted with a Scorpio, because at last they feel free to really let rip emotionally. However, the intuitive Cancerian should beware of soaking up the Scorpio's darker moods like a psychic sponge. A Cancerian will take one look at a delicate Piscean and want to invite them home for a good hot meal. All the Cancerian's protective instincts are aroused by a gentle Piscean, but their anger will also be aroused if it turns out the Piscean has been leading a double life behind their back.

Cancerians also find a great deal of comfort in the company of the Earth signs – Taurus, Virgo and Capricorn. Cancer and Taurus were made for each other – they both adore home comforts and they trust one another implicitly. The Cancerian loves making a cosy nest for their hard-working Taurean. A Cancerian finds a Virgo a more difficult proposition, especially emotionally. Whereas Cancer is all warm hugs and holding hands by the fire, Virgo prefers to read a book and reserve any displays of affection for the bedroom. Cancer and Capricorn are opposite numbers in the zodiac, so share a tremendous rapport. They also share the same values of home, tradition and family, and if anyone can help a Capricorn to relax and take life easy, it's a Cancerian.

Life becomes more difficult when it comes to a Cancerian's relationship with any of the Air signs. They simply don't understand one another. A Cancerian can't make a Gemini out. They feel confused by what they think of as the Gemini's flightiness and inability to stay in one place for long. They can also be easily hurt by the Gemini's difficulty in expressing their emotions. A Cancerian gets on much better with a Libran. They're both ambitious in their own ways and so have a great deal in common. The Cancerian enjoys the Libran's romantic nature, but the Cancerian tendency to cling doesn't go down well. A Cancerian regards a typical Aquarian as a being from another planet. They're hurt by the Aquarian's strong need for independence and dislike of having to account for their every action, and are dismayed and confused by the Aquarian's hot-and-cold attitude to sex.

The Fire signs of Aries, Leo and Sagittarius are also a potential source of bewilderment to the gentle Cancerian. They understand the drive and ambition of an Arien, but will be stung by their blunt speech and worried about their daredevil tendencies. What if they hurt themselves? A Cancerian gets on well with a Leo because they share a strong love of family and are both openly affectionate and loving. The Cancerian enjoys creating a home that the Leo can feel proud of. So far, so good, but the story isn't so simple when a Cancerian pairs up with a Sagittarian. They're too different to understand one another – the Cancerian wants to stay at home with the family while the Sagittarian has an instinctive need to roam the world. As a result, the Cancerian will be disappointed, and then hurt, when the Sagittarian's busy schedule takes them away from home too often.

Leo

Leos adore the company of their fellow Fire signs, Ariens and Sagittarius. They understand one another and enjoy each other's spontaneous warmth and affection. A Leo is amused by the exuberance and impulsiveness of an Arien, and they enjoy being persuaded to let their hair down a bit and not worry too much about appearances. A Leo enjoys the dash and vitality of a Sagittarian, although they may feel irritated if they can never get hold of them on the phone or the Sagittarian is always off doing other things. Two Leos together either love or loathe one another. One of them should be prepared to take a back seat, otherwise they'll both be vying for the limelight all the time.

The three Air signs of Gemini, Libra and Aquarius all get on well with Leos. When a Leo pairs up with a Gemini, you can expect lots of laughter and plenty of fascinating conversations. The demonstrative Leo is able to help the Gemini be more openly affectionate and loving. Leo and Libra is a great combination, and the Leo is enchanted by the Libran's fair-minded attitude. Both signs love luxury and all the good things in life but their bank managers may not be so pleased by the amount of the money they manage to spend. Leo and Aquarius sit opposite one another across the horoscope, so they already have a great deal in common. They're fascinated by one another but they're both very stubborn, so any disputes between them usually end in stalemate because neither is prepared to concede any ground.

Leos don't really understand the Earth signs. Although Leos admire their practical approach to life, they find it rather restricting. A Leo enjoys the sensuous and hedonistic side of a Taurean's character but may become frustrated by their fear of change. Leo and Virgo have very little in common, especially when it comes to food – the Leo wants to tuck in at all the best restaurants while the Virgo is worried about the state of the kitchens, the number of calories and the size of the bill. A Leo respects the Capricorn's desire to support their family and approves of their need to be seen in the best possible light, but they feel hurt by the Capricorn's difficulty in showing their feelings.

When a Leo gets together with one of the Water signs – Cancer, Scorpio or Pisces – they'll enjoy the sexual side of the relationship but could eventually feel stifled by all that Watery emotion. A Leo and a Cancerian adore making a home together and both dote on their children. The Leo also likes comforting their vulnerable Cancerian – provided this doesn't happen too often. A Leo and a Scorpio will be powerfully attracted to one another, but power could also pull them apart – who's going to wear the trousers? They'll also lock horns during rows and both of them will refuse to back down. A Leo delights in a sophisticated Piscean, but may become irritated by their indecision and jangly nerves.

 Virgo

As you might imagine, Virgos are happy with their fellow Earth signs of Taurus and Capricorn because they share the same practical attitude. A Virgo enjoys the steady, reassuring company of a Taurean, and they might even learn to relax a little instead of worrying themselves into the ground over the slightest problem. When two Virgos get together it can be too much of a good thing. Although at first they'll love talking to someone who shares so many of their preoccupations and ideas, they can soon drive one another round the bend. When a Virgo first meets a Capricorn they're delighted to know someone who's obviously got their head screwed on. It's only later on that they wish the Capricorn could lighten up every now and then.

Virgos get on well with Cancerians, Scorpios and Pisceans, the three Water signs. A Virgo enjoys being looked after by a considerate Cancerian, although they'll worry about their waistline and may get irritated by the Cancerian's super-sensitive feelings. You can expect plenty of long, analytical conversations when a Virgo gets together with a Scorpio. They both love getting to the bottom of subjects and will endlessly talk things through. They'll also get on extremely well in the bedroom. Pisces is Virgo's opposite sign, but although some opposites thrive in each other's company, that isn't always the case with this combination. The Virgo could soon grow impatient with the dreamy Piscean and will long to tell them a few home truths.

Although the other Earth signs don't usually get on well with Air signs, it's different for Virgos. They understand the intellectual energies of Geminis, Librans and Aquarians. A Virgo thrives in a Gemini's company, and they spend hours chatting over the phone if they can't get together in person. It's difficult for them to discuss their emotions, however, and they may never tell each other how they really feel. A Virgo admires a sophisticated, charming Libran, and marvels at their diplomacy. How do they do it? Expect a few sparks to fly when a Virgo pairs up with an Aquarian, because both of them have very strong opinions and aren't afraid to air them. The result is a lot of hot air and some vigorous arguments.

The three Fire signs – Aries, Leo and Sagittarius – are a source of endless fascination to a Virgo. They've got so much energy! A Virgo finds an Arien exciting but their relationship could be short-lived because the Virgo will be so irritated by the Arien's devil-may-care attitude to life. When a Virgo pairs up with a Leo, they'll be intrigued by this person's comparatively lavish lifestyle but their own modest temperament will be shocked if the Leo enjoys showing off. A Virgo is able to talk to a Sagittarius until the cows come home – they're both fascinated by ideas, although the precise Virgo will first be amused, and then irritated, by the Sagittarian's rather relaxed attitude to hard facts.

 Libra

Of all the members of the zodiac, this is the one that finds it easiest to get on with the other signs. Librans get on particularly well with Geminis and Aquarians, their fellow Air signs. A Libran is enchanted by a Gemini's quick brain and ready wit, and they enjoy endless discussions on all sorts of subjects. When two Librans get together, they revel in the resulting harmonious atmosphere but it's almost impossible for them to reach any decisions – each one defers to the other while being unable to say what they really want. A Libran is intrigued by the independence and sharp mind of an Aquarian, but their feelings could be hurt by the Aquarian's emotional coolness.

Libra enjoys being with the three Fire signs – Aries, Leo and Sagittarius. Libra, who often takes life at rather a slow pace, is energized by a lively Arien, and they complement one another's personalities well. However, the Libran may occasionally feel hurt by the Arien's single-mindedness and blunt speech. A Libran adores the luxury-loving ways of a Leo, and they'll both spend a fortune in the pursuit of happiness. They also get on well in the bedroom. When a Libran gets together with an exuberant Sagittarian, they'll have great fun. All the same, the Sagittarian need for honesty could fluster the Libran, who adopts a much more diplomatic approach to life.

Although the other two Air signs can find it hard to understand members of the Water element, it's different for Librans. They're more sympathetic to the emotional energies of Cancerians, Scorpios and Pisceans. A Libran delights in the protective care of a Cancerian, but those ever-changing Cancerians moods may be hard for a balanced Libran to take.

Those deep Scorpio emotions will intrigue the Libran but they may quickly become bogged down by such an intense outlook on life and will be desperate for some light relief. As for Pisces, the Libran is charmed by the Piscean's delicate nature and creative gifts, but both signs hate facing up to unpleasant facts so this couple may never deal with any problems that lie between them.

Libra enjoys the reliable natures of Taurus, Virgo and Capricorn, the Earth signs. A Libran appreciates the company of a relaxed and easy-going Taurean, although they may sometimes regret the Taurean's lack of imagination. When a Libran and a Virgo get together, the Libran enjoys the Virgo's mental abilities but their critical comments will soon cut the Libran to the quick. The Libran may not come back for a second tongue-lashing. A Libran understands the ambitions of a Capricorn, and likes their steady nature and the way they support their family. However, there could soon be rows about money, with the Libran spending a lot more than the Capricorn thinks is necessary.

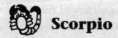

Scorpio

Not every sign gets on well with its fellow members, yet an astonishing number of Scorpios pair up. They feel safe together because they know the worst and best about each other. When things are good, they're brilliant but these two can also bring out the worst in each other, with intense silences and brooding sulks. A Scorpio enjoys the tender ministrations of a loving Cancerian, and adores being with someone who's so obviously concerned about their welfare. Feelings run deep when a Scorpio pairs up with a Piscean, although the Scorpio may become impatient with the Piscean's reluctance to face up to unpalatable truths.

The three Earth signs, Taurus, Virgo and Capricorn, are well-suited to the Scorpio temperament. Those astrological opposites, Scorpio and Taurus, enjoy a powerful relationship, much of which probably takes place in the bedroom, but whenever they have a disagreement there's an atmosphere you could cut with a knife, and neither of them will be prepared to admit they were in the wrong. A Scorpio is attracted to a neat, analytical Virgo but their feelings will be hurt by this sign's tendency to criticize. What's more, their pride stops them telling the Virgo how they feel. The Scorpio admires a practical Capricorn, especially if they've earned a lot of respect through their work, but this could be a rather chilly pairing because both signs find it difficult to show their feelings.

When you put a Scorpio together with one of the three Fire signs, they'll either get on famously or won't understand one another at all. A Scorpio revels in the lusty Arien's sex drive, although they'll soon feel tired if they try to keep up with the Arien's busy schedule. The combination of Scorpio and Leo packs quite a punch. They're both very strong personalities, but they boss one another around like mad and find it almost impossible to achieve a compromise if they fall out. A Scorpio likes to take life at a measured pace, so they're bemused by a Sagittarian's need to keep busy all the time. In the end, they'll become fed up with never seeing the Sagittarian, or playing second fiddle to all their other interests.

Scorpio is bemused by the three Air signs – Gemini, Libran and Aquarius – because they operate on such completely different wavelengths. A Scorpio can be good friends with a Gemini but they're at emotional cross-purposes, with the Scorpio's intense approach to life too much for a light-hearted Gemini to cope with. Emotions are also the bugbear between a Scorpio and a Libran. Everything is great at first, but the Scorpio's powerful feelings and dark moods will eventually send the Libran running in the opposite direction. You can expect some tense arguments when a Scorpio pairs up with an

Aquarian – they're both convinced that they're right and the other one is wrong.

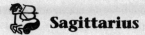 **Sagittarius**

When a Sagittarian pairs up with a fellow Fire sign, there's plenty of warmth and the odd firework. A Sagittarian is thrilled by the adventurous spirit of an Arien, and they love exploring the world together. There are plenty of tall tales when a Sagittarian gets together with a Leo – they'll try to outdo each other, dropping names and recounting their greatest triumphs. If the Leo is slightly pompous, the Sagittarian is able to take them down a peg or two, but they must beware of hurting the Leo's feelings. As for two Sagittarians, they'll spur each other on and encourage one another to gain as much experience of life as possible. You probably won't be able to move in their house for books.

With their endless curiosity about the world, Sagittarians understand the intellectual Air signs very well. A Sagittarian enjoys the chatty company of a Gemini and, because they're opposite numbers in the zodiac, the Sagittarian is able to encourage the Gemini to see things through and explore them in more detail than usual. A refined and diplomatic Libran will try to teach the blunt Sagittarian not to say the first thing that pops into their head. However, the Sagittarian may eventually find the Libran's sense of balance rather trying – why can't they get more worked up about things? There's plenty of straight talking when a Sagittarian teams up with an Aquarian – they both have a high regard for honesty. The independent Sagittarian respects the Aquarian's need for freedom, but may feel rather stung by their periods of emotional coolness.

A Sagittarian will struggle to understand the Earth signs. They respect the Taurean's ability to work hard but they're driven to distraction by their reluctance to make changes and break out of any ruts they've fallen into. A Sagittarian enjoys talking to a brainy Virgo, but their expansive and spontaneous nature could eventually be restricted by the Virgo's need to think things through before taking action. When a Sagittarian gets together with a Capricorn, it's a case of optimism versus pessimism. While the Sagittarian's glass is half-full, the Capricorn's is always half-empty, and this causes many rows and possibly some ill feeling.

There could be lots of misunderstandings when a Sagittarian gets involved with one of the Water signs. A Sagittarian needs a bigger social circle than their family, whereas a Cancerian is quite happy surrounded by kith and kin. The Sagittarian need for independence won't go down well, either. It's like oil and water when a Sagittarian pairs up with a Scorpio. The Sagittarian is the roamer of the zodiac, whereas the Scorpio wants them where they can see them, in case they're up to no good. All will be well if the Sagittarian gets together with a strong-minded Piscean. In fact, they'll really enjoy one another's company. A Piscean who's lost in a world of their own, however, will soon leave them cold.

Compatibility in Love and Sex at a glance

F / M	♈	♉	♊	♋	♌	♍	♎	♏	♐	♑	♒	♓
♈	8	5	9	7	9	4	7	8	9	7	7	3
♉	6	8	4	10	7	8	8	7	3	8	2	8
♊	8	2	7	3	8	7	9	4	9	4	9	4
♋	5	10	4	8	6	5	6	8	2	9	2	8
♌	9	8	9	7	7	4	9	6	8	7	9	6
♍	4	8	6	4	4	7	6	7	7	9	4	4
♎	7	8	10	7	8	5	9	6	9	6	10	6
♏	7	9	4	7	6	6	7	10	5	6	5	7
♐	9	4	10	4	9	7	8	4	9	6	9	5
♑	7	8	4	9	6	8	6	4	4	8	4	5
♒	8	6	9	4	9	4	9	6	8	7	8	2
♓	7	6	7	9	6	7	6	9	7	5	4	9

1 = the pits
10 = the peaks

Key

♈ – Aries
♉ – Taurus
♊ – Gemini
♋ – Cancer
♌ – Leo
♍ – Virgo

♎ – Libra
♏ – Scorpio
♐ – Sagittarius
♑ – Capricorn
♒ – Aquarius
♓ – Pisces

Compatibility in Friendship at a glance

F⟋M	♈	♉	♊	♋	♌	♍	♎	♏	♐	♑	♒	♓
♈	8	5	10	5	9	3	7	8	9	6	8	5
♉	6	9	6	10	7	8	7	6	4	9	3	9
♊	9	3	9	4	9	8	10	5	10	5	10	6
♋	6	9	4	9	5	4	6	9	4	10	3	9
♌	10	7	9	6	9	4	8	6	9	6	9	7
♍	5	9	8	4	4	8	5	8	8	10	5	6
♎	8	9	10	8	8	6	9	5	9	6	10	7
♏	7	8	5	8	7	7	6	9	4	5	6	8
♐	9	5	10	4	10	8	8	4	10	7	9	6
♑	6	9	5	10	6	6	5	5	4	9	5	6
♒	9	6	10	5	9	5	9	7	9	5	9	3
♓	6	7	6	10	6	8	7	9	8	6	4	10

1 = the pits
10 = the peaks

Key

♈ - Aries
♉ - Taurus
♊ - Gemini
♋ - Cancer
♌ - Leo
♍ - Virgo

♎ - Libra
♏ - Scorpio
♐ - Sagittarius
♑ - Capricorn
♒ - Aquarius
♓ - Pisces

HOBBIES AND THE STARS

What do you do in your spare time? If you're looking for some new interests to keep you occupied in 2000, read on to discover which hobbies are ideal for your Sun sign.

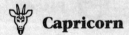 Capricorn

If you're a typical Capricorn you often take life rather seriously, so it's important for you to have lots of spare-time activities that allow you to relax. However, you've got to find the time first, and that means stopping work rather than burning the candle at both ends. Something that might appeal to you is rock-climbing, and you'll enjoy planning the strategy of how you're going to get to the top. Even a gentle walk amid mountain scenery does you a lot of good and helps you to relax. You're a very practical sign and you enjoy gardening. Not only does it help to ground you, you also like growing your own fruit and vegetables and then comparing the prices with those in the shops. Music helps you to unwind, and you'll love going to the opera or a glittering concert.

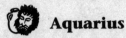 **Aquarius**

Most Aquarians have such a wide range of interests that almost anything is bound to appeal to you. You may go through phases, immersing yourself in one hobby for years until another one takes your fancy. However, you are only interested in activities that keep you intellectually stimulated and that teach you more about the world. You may go to lots of different evening classes, and you might even study for a degree in your spare time. Eastern philosophy could appeal, and you might also be an active campaigner for human rights. Astrology is a big hit with many Aquarians, and you'll enjoy teaching yourself all about it. Group activities are another interest, and you're an avid member of all sorts of organizations and societies.

 **Pisces**

Anything artistic or creative is perfect for you, because you have abundant gifts at your disposal. Painting, drawing, writing poetry and dancing are all classic Piscean pastimes. In fact, you may feel rather fed up or stifled when you can't express yourself creatively. When you want to escape from the world, you love going to the cinema or the theatre. You're a Water sign so you enjoy any activities connected with water, such as swimming or other forms of water sports. Many Pisceans enjoy gardening, and you'll especially like having some form of water feature in your garden even if it's very modest. You're very musical, and would enjoy learning to play an instrument if you can't already do so. You might also like using your psychic talents, perhaps by learning to read the tarot or runes.

Aries

Ariens love to keep active, so you aren't interested in any sort of hobby that's very sedentary or that keeps you glued to the sofa. You much prefer being kept busy, especially if it's out of doors. You also have a strong sense of adventure and a great love of speed, so one hobby that's right up your street is motor-racing. You might be lucky enough to be the driver, or you could be a spectator shouting yourself hoarse from the stands, but this is a sport you love. Speaking of sports, anything that's competitive and which threatens to knock the stuffing out of you will also suit you down to the ground. Rugby, football and baseball all fit the bill, and you might also enjoy martial arts and Eastern forms of exercise such as T'ai Chi.

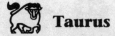 **Taurus**

You belong to one of the Earth signs, so it's no surprise that many Taureans were born with green fingers. You always feel better when you can be out in the fresh air, especially if you're in beautiful surroundings, so you adore gardening. Even if you're not keen on wielding a spade yourself you'll enjoy appreciating other people's efforts. Cooking is something that has enormous appeal for you and you enjoy creating gourmet meals, especially if the ingredients include your favourite foods. You also enjoy visiting swanky restaurants, although some of the gilt will be wiped off the gingerbread if you don't think you're getting value for money. Members of your sign are renowned for having beautiful voices so you might enjoy singing in a choir or on your own.

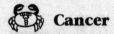 Gemini

One of your favourite ways of passing the time is to curl up with a good book. You'll eagerly read newspapers and magazines as well, and you always attempt crosswords and other sorts of puzzle even if you don't always finish them. Jigsaws intrigue you, especially if you can do something else at the same time, such as listening to music or watching the TV. You belong to a sign that doesn't like sitting still for long and you absolutely thrive on keeping active, so it's important for you to enjoy hobbies that make sure you get plenty of exercise. Tennis is a classic Gemini sport because it involves a lot of skill but it also boosts your social life. Dancing is another activity that helps you to keep fit while having a really good time.

Cancer

Home comforts are very important to you, so you spend a lot of time and money on making sure your home is the way you want it. You may enjoy reading magazines on interior design or you could be glued to all the DIY programmes on TV, adapting the best ideas for your own home. One of your greatest skills is cooking, because you belong to a sign that derives enormous emotional comfort from food. You take pleasure in cooking for your loved ones and you probably have a big collection of cookery books to provide you with endless inspiration. Water sports could appeal to you, especially if they involve visiting your favourite beach. You might also enjoy fishing, particularly if you can do it by moonlight.

Leo

You have a host of artistic skills and talents at your fingertips because you belong to the one of the most creative signs in the zodiac. One of your favourite hobbies is amateur dramatics, because most Leos adore being in the limelight. You may even have thought about becoming a professional actor because you enjoy treading the boards so much. You might also enjoy dancing, whether you go to regular classes or you simply love tripping the light fantastic with your partner. Travel appeals to you, especially if you can visit luxurious hotels in hot parts of the world. However, you're not very keen on roughing it! Clothes are very important to you, so you enjoy shopping for the latest fashions and you may also be an accomplished dressmaker.

 Virgo

One of your favourite pastimes is to keep up to date with your health. You're fascinated by medical matters and you enjoy reading books telling you how to keep fit. You may even try out all the latest eating regimes, hoping that you'll find one that suits you perfectly. This interest in health means you're keen to eat well, and you could enjoy growing your own vegetables. Even cultivating a few herbs in a windowbox will give you a sense of achievement and you'll be pleased to think they are doing you good. You have tremendous patience so you might enjoy fiddly hobbies that require great dexterity, such as knitting, needlepoint and sewing. You might also enjoy painting designs on china and glass.

Libra

Libra is a very sensual sign, so any hobbies that appeal to your senses are bound to go down well. You love delicious smells so you might enjoy learning about aromatherapy, so you can cure yourself of minor ailments and also create your own bath oils. You could also get a big thrill out of making your own cosmetics or soaps, and you might become so good at them that you give them away as gifts. You take great pride in looking good, so you enjoy visiting your favourite shops and keeping up with the latest fashions. Music is one of your great loves and you might play an instrument or sing. If not, you certainly appreciate other people's musical talents and you enjoy going to concerts and recitals.

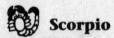 **Scorpio**

Whatever hobbies you choose, they have to mean a lot to you. You simply aren't interested in activities that don't carry an emotional meaning for you and you'd rather not bother with them at all. One pastime that's dear to the hearts of most Scorpios is wine-tasting. You might enjoy teaching yourself all about wine, either with the help of some good books or simply by drinking whatever appeals to you. You're fascinated by mysteries, and you could enjoy reading lots of whodunits or books on true crimes. You are also intrigued by things that go bump in the night, and you can't resist going on ghost hunts or visiting famous places that are known to be haunted.

Sagittarius

You're one of the great collectors of the zodiac, whether you know it or not. You may not think that you collect anything at all, but other people will take one look at all your books and beg to disagree with you. Reading is one of your great pleasures in life and you're always buying books on your latest enthusiasms. Travel is something else that appeals to you, and you love planning where you're going to go next on holiday. You like to keep active and you enjoy outdoor sports in particular. Horse-riding is a classic Sagittarian activity, and you enjoy going to the races and having a little flutter. You also like activities that present you with a challenge – you're always determined to beat it!

THE YEAR 2000

Friends and Lovers

The more work and effort you put into your loving relationships this year, the more you'll get out of them. That may not sound like a very romantic recipe but it will be a successful one. This is especially true if a close relationship goes through the doldrums in 2000. Rather than throwing in the towel at the first hint of trouble, it will be far better to grit your teeth, find out what's wrong and then set about trying to fix it. You will learn a lot from experience, which is one of your greatest Capricorn characteristics. This is also a year in which you will take your love life a lot more seriously than usual. That might be because something very important happens between you and a certain person, making it a year to remember, or you might simply want to channel a lot of energy into your loving relationships.

As the year begins, you are still enjoying a very happy phase in your domestic and family life. It's a joy to be with your nearest and dearest in the first six weeks of the year, and you may have very good reason to feel pleased with the way things are going at home. Between February and late June, you should grab every opportunity to have a really good time. You'll feel much more happy-go-lucky than usual, so make the most of it! Throw yourself into the social swing whenever you get the chance, especially if you're currently a single Capricorn but you want to find a new love. Cupid could strike when you're at a party, celebration or some other social setting. You might even find that you're spoilt for choice and that several prospective lovers have got their eye on you! If so, you may have to choose between someone with a lot of spending power and someone who makes you feel glad to be alive. Which one will you go for? You're going to have a lot of fun in 2000!

Health

It's a year for living it up and enjoying yourself, which is great news for your social life but may not be quite such glad tidings for your waistline! Even so, this is the year in which you can finally unwind and give yourself a break, especially if you were very busy in 1999 and you could now do with a breather. Holidays, weekends away and short breaks will all do you the world of good this year, not only because you'll enjoy having a change of scene but also because you will value having the time off to do other things. Having a wide range of interests and sparetime activities will also help you to unwind and relax.

You may have a tendency to overdo the food and drink between February and June, but you will certainly enjoy yourself at the same time. If you suspect that you're starting to put on weight, try to whittle away the pounds by keeping active. Competitive sports could appeal, but you will also benefit from taking brisk walks in lovely surroundings and these will help to keep you fit and well. If you feel liverish at times, give yourself a break from alcohol and rich foods until you feel better.

There will be times this year when your work keeps you fully occupied, and it may even eat into your spare time. If this happens, try not to burn the candle at both ends too often, because overworking will eventually drain you of energy. You might also be prone to bouts of worry and anxiety this year, especially between August and October, and this could cause sleepless nights or make you feel under par. If you start to experience any strange health symptoms, it will be much better to have a medical check-up than to struggle on alone, hoping that they will go away. If fears or worries start to prey on your mind, try to confide in someone or seek some form of professional help, otherwise you might find it difficult to switch off.

 **Money**

Your sign is not usually noted for its spendthrift tendencies, but you are definitely starting to feel the urge to splurge. This will be especially strong between February and June, when you long to throw caution to the winds and to scatter credit cards in all directions. You will be very tempted to spend money on luxuries, indulgences and treats, and if you can afford them there will be no stopping you. It's a wonderful excuse to spend money on yourself, especially if you fancy updating your image, adding to your wardrobe or buying yourself some presents. A busy social life could also make some hefty dents in your bank balance but you'll thoroughly enjoy yourself in the process.

Whether or not you spend a lot of money in 2000, it is important that you keep your feet on the ground when tackling your finances. You may be surprised to read this advice because you do not usually need to hear it, being one of the most practical signs of the zodiac. However, you may succumb to an uncharacteristic tendency to turn a blind eye to unpleasant financial facts in 2000. For instance, if you receive a nasty letter from your bank manager you might ignore it, or you could go on a big spending spree when you know you can't afford it. If you do play fast and loose with your money, or run into debt, you may have to cope with the consequences in July and August.

Even so, this is a marvellous year for buying items that will give you pleasure or improve the quality of your life, provided you can afford them. If you do have the money to spare, you will want to buy items that are high quality, built to last and that will make you look good.

Career

It's a mixed year where your career is concerned. You will benefit in many ways from expressing your talents and skills, but this is also a year in which you will have to keep your nose to the grindstone at times. In fact, the year divides neatly in two. Between January and June is the best time to enjoy using your creative abilities. After that, you will become increasingly busy at work.

This is certainly a great opportunity to make the most of

your gifts and abilities, especially if you enjoy expressing them. Bring out your creative and artistic talents in any way you can. You might even be given the chance to earn money through one of your skills, so it isn't a year for false modesty or keeping your gifts to yourself. Instead, you should be prepared to take a chance or stick your neck out at times. Something else to consider is developing new abilities. Just because you haven't yet tried something does not mean you won't be any good at it, so don't be shy about experimenting with different things.

If your career already involves being creative or artistic, you can expect some bumper opportunities between January and August. You could get the chance to consolidate the progress that you've made so far, or you might finally receive the rewards that have eluded you for so long.

The second half of the year will have plenty to keep you occupied at work. You may be asked to step into the breach and cover for a colleague, or you could be given extra responsibilities and duties. There will be times when you feel you are working round the clock for little or no reward. Although it won't do your self-esteem much good to feel that your efforts are not appreciated, are you sure this is the case? You may not receive many pats on the back, but you will prove that you're an invaluable person to have around.

Your Day by Day Guide

JANUARY AT A GLANCE

Love	♥ ♥ ♥ ♥ ♥
Money	£ $ £ $ £
Career	💻 💻 💻
Health	☼ ☼ ☼ ☼ ☼

• *Saturday 1 January* •

Happy New Year! Luckily, you're starting the New Year feeling self-assured and in a position of strength. While everyone else is recovering from the festive season's excesses, you're feeling fighting fit and ready to take on the world. This is an excellent day to decide exactly what it is you want to achieve this year. Then you can put your plans into action and be on the way to realizing a life-long ambition.

• *Sunday 2 January* •

You need to find a way of letting off steam today as some things may not go as smoothly as they're supposed to. Although you normally pride yourself on your self-control, an old grievance that you've been harbouring could get to you and make you lose your rag. This really is a perfect opportunity to clear any old skeletons from the cupboard and resolve a long-standing issue once and for all.

• *Monday 3 January* •

Yesterday may have been a storm in a teacup but the waters could still feel a little choppy. Only by keeping a sense of perspective can you hope to navigate a smooth passage through the emotional minefield around you. Just how strongly you feel about a certain situation is now patently obvious, but you're at a loss as to how to express yourself. Allow your intuition to guide you.

• *Tuesday 4 January* •

The pace of your everyday life is about to change gear. Your mental energy level is being charged up and giving you the opportunity of a brand new perspective. Provided you are willing to be more flexible and open in the way you communicate your new ideas, you'll be delightfully surprised by the reception they get. The softly-softly approach, rather than the hard sell, will work wonders.

• *Wednesday 5 January* •

Your emotional radar system is turned full on today and you're feeling particularly sensitive to the moods of those around you. Someone may need your sympathy and understanding, and your common sense and practical nature will offer them exactly the support they need. Make sure that you help them to help themselves rather than allow them to depend on you for all the answers.

• *Thursday 6 January* •

You are now in a position to start cutting out all the dead wood from your life and to make some decisive moves towards those important goals you've set your sights on. You will be firing on all cylinders during the coming fortnight so don't allow yourself to be distracted. Once you've committed to something you have the power to move mountains. The stage is set, and all you have to do now is call 'action'!

• *Friday 7 January* •

You are definitely feeling good about yourself, and this renewed self-confidence and optimism thrusts you into a flurry of activity today. You will be able on rely on getting a lot of support from the people around you. It's also a great day for spending some money on your home and family, especially if you fancy a trip around the January sales to see what's on offer.

• *Saturday 8 January* •

You have been so preoccupied recently that it's no surprise if you haven't been able to keep track of your finances. You may be about to discover that they aren't in as good a shape as you thought they were. However small the difference is between what you thought you had in the bank and what there is in reality, it may be enough to send you into a panic. Aren't you overreacting slightly?

• *Sunday 9 January* •

Hold tight, because you're about to have a reminder that you aren't in complete control over certain elements of your life. If you are looking for cast-iron assurances of your future security, remind yourself of how much you've achieved already. If you really want to strengthen your position, learn the difference between what you can change and what you can't. When you've worked that out, you'll have a whole new perspective on what is possible.

• *Monday 10 January* •

It will be awfully easy to get yourself in a right old state today and to let rip whenever you feel angry or irritated. A certain person has got right up your nose, but are you justified in having such a paddy? Although you need to tell this person if you don't like their current behaviour, it may not be such a good idea to let off steam in quite such a spectacular manner. You may have to backtrack once you have calmed down!

• Tuesday 11 January •

Confused? You seem to be communicating at cross-purposes with someone and not saying what you really feel. A relative or close friend may try to persuade you to follow a certain course of action and you'll find yourself going along with it unless you speak up in time. The irony is that they believe they have your best interests at heart, but in reality you would be wise to follow your own hunches.

• Wednesday 12 January •

If you have been in two minds about how committed you are to someone, you can at last begin to put your relationship on a more solid footing. You are feeling the need for greater permanency and both you and your partner now need to know where you stand. Your personal happiness is being highlighted and it's time to let your loved one know how you feel.

• Thursday 13 January •

Whatever else you do today, try to set aside some time to do some housework. This may not make you want to rush off and immediately grab a duster, but you will enjoy making your home look neat and tidy. It will be good therapy to get rid of all the clutter that you have amassed recently. An added bonus will be the gratitude shown to you by the rest of the family!

• Friday 14 January •

If you want to make a positive impact on the world, this is the day to do it. Capitalize on your bold self-assurance to break the mould and inject new life into areas that have gone stale. You really can't afford to hold yourself back any longer, so go on, ring the changes and enjoy the results. You'll find that the people you have been trying to win over will suddenly see you in a new light.

• *Saturday 15 January* •

You are definitely in your element whenever you are faced with a challenge, and more often than not you are able to turn situations round to your advantage. You have certainly emerged stronger and wiser from all the changes that have taken place recently. All you have to do now is to tie up the loose ends so that you can concentrate on developing a more secure base of operations.

• *Sunday 16 January* •

Being clear and direct in your dealings with others may put people's backs up but at least they will know where they stand with you and exactly what your objectives are. Today is one of those days where your mind is working overtime and others may struggle to keep up with you. You're problem-solving at the speed of light and you should remind yourself that not everyone has your mental agility.

• *Monday 17 January* •

Are you baffled about someone's behaviour? If so, it's probably because you're sending them mixed messages. It's no good pretending that everything is OK when you're seething with resentment underneath. Put your feelings on the line and say what's irritating you. This may cause a few fireworks, but at least you will be able to clear up any misunderstandings and . air your grievances.

• *Tuesday 18 January* •

Watch out for power struggles today because you could be locking horns with a close relative or neighbour. How important this issue is to you will ultimately determine whether you stick to your guns or back down. One thing's for sure, you've certainly met your match and any confrontation will test the courage of your convictions. Weigh up all the odds before you go into battle mode.

• *Wednesday 19 January* •

Do you ever really take the time to acknowledge your abilities and positive qualities? Whatever your answer is, the coming few weeks are an excellent chance to evaluate your strengths. Two of your greatest attributes are your business acumen and negotiating skills. These could soon be put to the test and you will have to make sure that everyone benefits equally from any financial deal you make.

• *Thursday 20 January* •

Don't expect to come up with all the answers today! You're not thinking straight and you have a tendency to daydream and let the day drift by. The good news is that you will find it easy to look at things in a more flexible and open-minded way than usual. The bad news is that you could be deluding yourself in some way. Don't commit yourself to anything important until you are more sure of your ground.

• *Friday 21 January* •

Today's Full Moon brings to a head an emotive situation that has been brewing for some time now. Your best bet is to face the music over the next two weeks and to work out your differences as best you can. If the root of the problem is a dispute over joint finances, it is highly likely that one of you is pushing for greater control. Getting a third party to assess the situation may be the only way to avoid reaching a deadlock.

• *Saturday 22 January* •

Are you bored with your everyday life? You won't be this weekend when you should expect the unexpected. There's no point in trying to plan anything so you might as well break with your routine and do something completely different. It's not often that you can afford to be this spontaneous, so give yourself a free rein and dare to be different. You never know, you might even enjoy it!

• Sunday 23 January •

If you have managed to get off the beaten track this weekend, make sure you get plenty of exercise and blow away the cobwebs. Getting rid of your inertia will boost your energy levels and give you a new lease of life. If you have opted to stay in familiar surroundings, you can still put your mind to work and come up with a plan to inject new life into your established routine. Go for it!

• Monday 24 January •

Good news! Your popularity rating starts to shoot up from today, and over the next few weeks you will be in great demand when it comes to social events. What's more, you will be blessed with an extra dose of charm and diplomacy, making you the natural magnet of everyone around you. If you are currently single, you might soon attract someone who definitely has designs on your heart.

• Tuesday 25 January •

It will be easy to press the panic button and imagine the worst today, especially if you are tackling anything connected with your finances or your love life. You could also be upset by the chilly atmosphere between you and a certain person. Although it will be tempting to think that this means the writing is on the wall for the two of you, it is much more likely to be a temporary blip that will soon blow over.

• *Wednesday 26 January* •

You can charm the birds off the trees today, and your popularity rating is about to go through the roof in your professional life. Because you're able to do such a good PR job on yourself, you can't help but win people over to your way of thinking. Part of your successful strategy lies in your ability to listen to other people's opinions and yet still convince them of the brilliance of your own ideas.

• *Thursday 27 January* •

Everyone wants a piece of you today, which leaves you somewhat fragmented. You feel torn between spending time with a family member and helping someone at work to resolve a difficult issue. Either way, there isn't enough of you to go round. Maybe the lesson here is that you can't be all things to all people and that you can't always be the one to take on responsibility for other people's problems.

• *Friday 28 January* •

Where is everyone when you need them? If you are feeling lonely or depressed, ask yourself why. Could it be that you give the impression of being totally self-sufficient and you don't allow others to help? Remember that you're human and need emotional support just as much as everyone else. Allow yourself to feel vulnerable and, if necessary, to ask someone for their support.

• *Saturday 29 January* •

You're in a state of flux today and are likely to change your mind more than once over a particular issue. The trouble is that you can't decide whether to let your head or your heart take charge. No wonder you don't know which way to turn! One thing is clear – you have a strong need to express how you feel. So take a deep breath, collect yourself and take the plunge.

• *Sunday 30 January* •

'Know yourself and the truth shall set you free' is an age-old adage that contains a lot of wisdom. Do you really know yourself as well as you think you do? You could be about to discover a couple of blind spots that it's time you became aware of. Once you've identified them, a burden that you've been carrying will miraculously lift. And then you will discover a lighter side to your personality that you never knew about before.

• *Monday 31 January* •

All the introspection that you've indulged in recently has allowed a few chinks in your armour to show through. Paradoxically, this can only help you to gain greater confidence in yourself because you are no longer trying to be a tower of strength for everyone else. Your highly developed sense of duty and responsibility to others is admirable, but are you taking your own needs into account? If not, maybe it's time to start?

FEBRUARY AT A GLANCE

Love	♥ ♥ ♥
Money	£ $ £ $ £
Career	💻 💻 💻
Health	☼ ☼ ☼ ☼

• *Tuesday 1 February* •

Hold tight – you're about to experience life without a safety net! You're in such a positive mood today that others can't help but feel uplifted by being around you. What you are glimpsing is the prospect of a bigger, better future, so it's not surprising that you're ready to try something new. Although you often prefer to play it safe, that is the last thing on your mind right now. This time you're going for broke!

• Wednesday 2 February •

Heave a deep sigh of relief! It looks as though your gamble paid off and you can revel in the feeling of having broken your own rules and come up trumps. What you didn't really count on was the show of support you received. Isn't it good to know that everyone is rooting for you and that you don't have to go it alone? There's a lot more to be gained than you realized from joining forces with others.

• Thursday 3 February •

You have no doubts about where you stand now and neither does anybody else. You're in the enviable position of being able to call the shots without having to force any issues. Not everyone masters the art of being a good leader as well as knowing how to be a team player, so it's about time you gave yourself a pat on the back for pulling off such a tricky combination.

• Friday 4 February •

Trust your instincts today, even if logic wants to take the upper hand. This is especially important where your finances and home life are concerned. If you normally see things in black and white, you could find that there's a much wider spectrum of possibilities than you'd thought. It's a great day for buying something to improve the look or comfort of your home.

• Saturday 5 February •

Be prepared to be swept along by events from today – things will be moving so fast that you'll hardly have time to come up

for air. Your mind is being bombarded with new and innovative ideas that are coming from out of the blue and over
which you seem to have no control. Make sure you write down
your thoughts or they're liable to evaporate and then you
really will kick yourself.

• *Sunday 6 February* •

Anyone coming into your orbit today is likely to receive an
electric shock from the static you're generating! You've got no
time to sit around and watch the grass grow – you want action.
You can tackle just about anything you set your mind to
today, especially if it has connections with your finances. You
could make some innovative changes that are long overdue
and which will transform your money matters for the better.

• *Monday 7 February* •

Gravity has pulled you back to earth and you need some time
alone today to be calm and reflective. Once you've collected
yourself, get together with someone that you trust and respect
because they will make a great sounding board. Talk about
your feelings or discuss a current difficulty, especially if you
can't see the wood for the trees. A heart-to-heart with someone will soon help you to put things in perspective.

• *Tuesday 8 February* •

Keep a grip on your temper today! In fact, you're ready to fly
off the handle at the slightest provocation. Try to sort out
what's bugging you, otherwise you're likely to upset the very
people that you've worked so hard to establish a good relationship with. Calm down and don't take things quite so seriously.
You do have a sense of humour, remember?

• *Wednesday 9 February* •

You are in a very dreamy mood today and will much prefer to drift along at your own pace than to keep up with everyone else. Ideally, you should absent yourself from the usual hurly-burly and tuck yourself away at home instead. It will be lovely if you can gather some of your nearest and dearest around you, or perhaps you would prefer to cuddle up with you-know-who?

• *Thursday 10 February* •

You are feeling very light-hearted and sociable, so why not have open house and invite everyone over to your place? You are in the mood to entertain, so any party you throw today is guaranteed to go with a swing. This is a wonderful time to get together with old friends that you don't often have a chance to see, even if it can't be on home territory.

• *Friday 11 February* •

You are probably feeling slightly the worse for wear today, especially if you were very sociable yesterday, and it won't be easy to concentrate on what you're supposed to be doing. You would much rather take it easy and relax, so it's almost an impossible task to discipline yourself and perform your duties. All you can do is pace yourself and draw on your considerable reserves of stamina to see you through.

• *Saturday 12 February* •

You've got the bit between your teeth again and you'll be raring to go during the next few weeks. Your energy levels have picked up so dramatically that you're liable to overdo it if you're not careful. Take a few deep breaths before you go into overdrive and you'll feel a lot calmer. There's no stopping you when you've set yourself a challenge but you will be much more productive if you can shift down a gear.

• *Sunday 13 February* •

Something is nagging away at you and you can't quite put your finger on what it is. You're determined to get to the root of this feeling but it will be awfully easy to turn this quest into an obsession and end up feeling mentally exhausted. Try switching your attention to something else because that will help the answer to pop into your mind.

• *Monday 14 February* •

Make sure that you say what you mean and mean what you say today, otherwise Valentine's Day is likely be fraught with misunderstandings. The problem is that you're having difficulty in making up your mind and deciding exactly where your true affections lie. Your heart says one thing and your head says another, which explains why you're giving mixed messages. Perhaps you need to do some serious thinking?

• *Tuesday 15 February* •

If you've been feeling physically under par recently, so that everything has taken more of an effort than usual, you will be pleased to know that your vitality is now beginning to return. Between now and late June you will want to throw yourself into life at full tilt, and there will certainly be a lot to smile about. A new love might come along or you could get a kick out of expressing some of your talents that have lain dormant until now. Enjoy yourself!

• *Wednesday 16 February* •

You get a valuable insight today into what makes your close relationships tick – and not before time! Someone is about to give you some very positive feedback about their feelings for you, and you are likely to respond in kind. You so often hold yourself in check but this is one occasion when you can allow yourself to put your feelings into words and let yourself go.

• *Thursday 17 February* •

If you have been feeling the financial pinch recently, all that could soon change. Over the next few weeks you might receive a large bonus or a windfall that you didn't expect. Either way, the financial picture will look a lot more rosy than it has done recently. If you want to make absolutely sure that you are making the most of your money, double-check your investments to make sure they are performing well.

• *Friday 18 February* •

If you are the sort of Capricorn who usually thinks twice before shelling out your cash, don't be surprised if you are overtaken by a deliciously extravagant streak today. You could splash out on all sorts of treats and luxuries, whether you need them or not. In fact, the more hedonistic or pampering they are, the more drawn to them you will be. You will have fun spending money but try not to go overboard unless you know you can afford it.

• *Saturday 19 February* •

Don't leave people in the dark during the coming fortnight. Any little tensions that have been brewing could explode into World War III unless you defuse the situation by saying what's on your mind. Part of the problem is that you're trying to stick to the same old routine when actually you've become bored with the status quo. This is making you feel both restless and frustrated, so maybe it's time you did something about it.

• *Sunday 20 February* •

Local events and neighbourhood activities could keep you very busy between now and mid-March. They might even introduce you to a new set of friends or help you to explore new parts of your local environment. If you have been having problems with a neighbour or someone you see on a regular basis, this will be a good opportunity to put matters to rights.

• *Monday 21 February* •

You are mounting a major charm offensive today and it looks as though everyone will be seduced by such a winning strategy. If you have to give a talk or presentation, you'll have no problem in convincing even the most hard-nosed customer that what you say is right. They'll probably wind up thinking that it was their idea in the first place, but that won't bother you. You will know what really happened!

• *Tuesday 22 February* •

Do you fancy giving yourself a treat? Then try to make some time today for whatever or whoever makes your world go round. Concentrating on something that has tremendous meaning for you will remind you of the good things in life, and will also give you a big emotional charge. It's not a good day to buy anything expensive because you could easily be persuaded to part with money against your better judgement.

• *Wednesday 23 February* •

You are about to set the cat among the pigeons because you simply cannot pull your punches. Fortunately, this will probably work in your favour, especially if you air your views about a career or financial matter. The general consensus of opinion may be that you're mad but, if you dare to stick to your guns, everyone will thank you in the end.

• *Thursday 24 February* •

It's a wonderful day for being sociable because you will revel in the company of friends and loved ones. You don't have to do anything very ambitious or energetic, because simply enjoying the company of certain people will be more than enough for you. A group activity will go very well, especially if you are going along for the first time and are feeling nervous. You'll have a lot of fun!

• Friday 25 February •

An unexpected turn of events sheds new light on a certain situation today. You might discover something new about a friend or you could receive a shock about your finances. Should you blow a fuse and run the risk of alienating everyone concerned or should you tackle the situation head-on but still keep your cool? Try to think before you speak, even though it will be tempting to say the first thing that comes into your head.

• Saturday 26 February •

To a large extent, your mood today will be determined by how successfully you managed to sort out yesterday's problem. You could either feel elated and as if a weight has been taken off your shoulders, or you might be confused and vaguely anxious. If you are feeling positive, you can rest assured that you've gained more than you've lost and that the experience will prove to be invaluable.

• Sunday 27 February •

You are in one of those deliciously sensual moods where all you want to do is curl up with a certain person and let nature take its course. Shutting out the rest of the world will do you the power of good, and it will improve your love life no end! If you don't have anyone who fits the bill, channel your energies into being busy around the house, especially if you fancy doing some decorating or gardening.

• *Monday 28 February* •

You could be feeling the pinch today because you seem to be spending money faster than you are getting it. The chances are that you will decide to tighten your control on your outgoings and lead a more frugal life for the time being, but making a resolution is one thing and keeping it is another! You're much more likely to make a token gesture towards scaling down your spending than to initiate a full-blown economy drive.

• *Tuesday 29 February* •

As a Capricorn, you have an enviable reputation for being someone who can be relied on. This can cause problems at times but today you are more than happy to let someone pick your brains or seek your advice. You will do your utmost to give them your support. If there have been problems between you and a certain someone recently, have a few quiet words in their ear now and see if you can find a solution.

MARCH AT A GLANCE

Love	❤ ❤ ❤ ❤ ❤
Money	£ $ £ $
Career	💻 💻 💻
Health	☼ ☼ ☼

• *Wednesday 1 March* •

You're on a fact-finding mission today and you need to gather as much information as possible to get the whole picture. Your nose is twitching which means you're more willing to let your intuition guide you instead of allowing logic and reason to dictate. On no account allow yourself to be pressured into making a decision you're not ready to make.

• *Thursday 2 March* •

You are in a very practical and organized mood today, so it's great for getting things done. Map out your strategy in advance so you don't waste any time. You will also find it easy to get other people motivated, which is good news if you are taking charge in some way. A neighbour or close relative may need your help, in which case you will be glad to do what you can.

• *Friday 3 March* •

Are you holding on to something that you no longer really need? This is a day to have a look at your belongings and decide whether any have outlived their usefulness. Perhaps you can't even remember when you last used some of the things or maybe you have a drawer full of clothes you are unlikely to wear again. It all boils down to keeping the things that you truly value and chucking out what you have kept out of habit.

• *Saturday 4 March* •

If you're going shopping today you might be tempted to buy something a little different, maybe even a little risqué! This is a good indication that you're now ready to change your image and experiment with the way you look. Even if you simply end up choosing bolder colours rather having than a total overhaul of your wardrobe, you will be delighted with the effect.

• *Sunday 5 March* •

Do you want to give yourself a treat? Then why not do something that you've wanted to do for ages but haven't got round to. It could be visiting a place you've been curious about and would love to explore, or dropping in on someone that you don't see very often. Doing things on the spur of the moment may not be your normal style but it could be a lot of fun now.

• *Monday 6 March* •

Are you keeping abreast of the latest technology or do you feel that you're lagging along in the slow lane? If you would like to improve your communications in some way, whether that means buying yourself a new alarm clock or launching yourself into cyberspace, the coming fortnight is an excellent time to start. It will also be a good opportunity to have an important conversation with you-know-who.

• *Tuesday 7 March* •

Have you got any DIY jobs left unfinished? You'll be amazed at how much you could get done today if you set your mind to it. You're probably better off working alone as you will only be irritated by someone else's shortcomings and they will slow you down. Just make sure that you don't take any short cuts because any mistakes you make could prove to be expensive.

• *Wednesday 8 March* •

Woe betide anyone who crosses you today as they're likely to get their head bitten off! This would be a great day to go to the gym and burn off some of that excess energy that's churning away inside you. The best cure is prevention, so next time you can feel yourself getting wound up, find some physical outlet to help diffuse the stress. Remember that letting off steam early can often prevent a volcanic eruption later on!

• *Thursday 9 March* •

Isn't it about time you spoilt yourself? Allow yourself a day of indulgence and get ready to be pampered. Why not enjoy a sensuous massage or an extravagant, delicious meal? Whatever you do, squeeze every drop of enjoyment out of the experience and take delight in life's luxuries. It's not every day that you give yourself permission for such hedonism, so make the most of it!

• Friday 10 March •

Oh dear! You're probably feeling horribly guilty about yesterday's pursuit of pleasure and furiously checking your bank balance. It's just as well that you are feeling flush at the moment, so there is no reason to panic. Once you have reassured yourself that you can still keep body and soul together and that the odd treat isn't a bad thing, you will realize that it feels good to spoil yourself every now and then.

• Saturday 11 March •

You're in two minds about whether to stay with what you know or whether to try something different today. Although the tried and tested path is a safe bet, you're intrigued by the unknown possibilities that the new direction holds. Don't rush the decision-making process. Instead, give yourself some time to mull over your options. In the end, you'll know exactly which way to go.

• Sunday 12 March •

You could feel as though you're being pulled in several different directions today because everyone is demanding something different from you. What's more, they expect you to deliver. Your only solution is to try to negotiate with them and reach some kind of compromise. It's not that you aren't able to come up with the goods, it's more that you should consider your own needs as well as everyone else's.

• *Monday 13 March* •

Over the next few weeks you will start climbing the walls if you have to spend too long in one place. You have a mild case of itchy feet and the last thing you will want is to feel bored or restless. So if you find yourself pacing up and down or feeling hemmed in, take yourself off for a walk or try to skip your usual routine. Once you have satisfied your desire to roam, you will be able to carry on with the daily chores.

• *Tuesday 14 March* •

It's all systems go today and everything can finally move forward again. You've had to deal with many uncertainties over the past few weeks, with some people being unreliable. This has taken its toll but at least now you're back on track. If communications have been scrambled or someone got the wrong end of the stick, you will now be able to start sorting things out and getting them back on an even keel.

• *Wednesday 15 March* •

It may be the middle of the week but how about planning something nicely romantic with you-know-who? However, you will have to switch off from more mundane matters first, otherwise you may find that you are gazing into space thinking about the washing while your partner is gazing into your eyes and wondering what's gone wrong. You could have an unexpected visitor.

• *Thursday 16 March* •

You've got a bee in your bonnet today and you're not budging from your position, no matter what. Are you refusing to back down out of principle, or are you too proud to give in? Even if you're convinced that you're in the right, being so inflexible won't do you any favours. It would be far better to discuss the problem with the people concerned and then reassess the situation in light of what you hear.

• Friday 17 March •

You must have got out of bed on the wrong side yesterday. You're much more interested today in finding a peaceful solution to any problems rather than mounting a full-scale offensive. Adopting a more tolerant tactic is more likely to persuade others of the value and merit of your ideas. And you too can benefit enormously from listening to what other people think.

• Saturday 18 March •

Cool, calm and collected is the best way to describe you today. You can take comfort from knowing that you are being true to yourself, and the deep sense of well-being and quiet contentment that you feel is proof of that. This is one of those days when you can simply go with the flow, confident in the knowledge that everything will run smoothly. Even if there are any hiccups, these won't even ruffle your feathers.

• Sunday 19 March •

You're all set to scale another mountain and meet the next challenge today. All this vim and vigour is bound to rub off on other people, because you will inspire both faith and confidence in everyone. So what are you going to do with this burst of new life? If you're a true-to-type Capricorn you'll probably pick the most daunting task you can think of but, by the same token, you're more than likely to get to the top.

• Monday 20 March •

A belief or philosophy that you set great store by could be challenged by the events that take place during the coming fortnight. You may have to rethink something that has always seemed to be second nature until now, or you might even realize that you have outgrown a particular code of conduct. You may also have to make some important decisions about an educational or travel matter.

• *Tuesday 21 March* •

Someone fairly influential could give you a lucky break today. This could take the form of a promotion or it might give you the opportunity to be more high-profile. This is your chance to sell yourself and to prove how well equipped you are for your next career move. It seems that you are the right person for the right job at the right time!

• *Wednesday 22 March* •

Something is stirring you up and you're feeling quite emotional. A friend who claims to have your best interests at heart may have said something that upset you and you don't know what to do about it. You're not in the most forgiving of moods and the trust between you may be beyond repair. Wait until you've calmed down before you make any definite decisions.

• *Thursday 23 March* •

No matter how hard you try, nothing seems to gel today and you probably feel like giving up altogether and going back to bed. Although you're no stranger to uphill battles, you can still have your moments of frustration and disillusionment. However, one of your strengths is that you somehow always manage to turn problems into situations that you can learn from, and you will get another chance to do that today.

• Friday 24 March •

Is the glass half full or half empty? The pessimist and the optimist in you are jostling for priority. Capricorns tend to be realistic rather than idealistic, but you're more in favour of looking on the bright side today in spite of your innate caution. So, if you have a hunch that it will pay off to see things in a positive light, go with that feeling and trust it.

• Saturday 25 March •

This is a wonderful day to have some time to yourself, so you can listen to music or read an inspirational book. Or maybe you would prefer to unwind by jogging round the park for a couple of hours? Either way, you need to recharge your batteries, and what better way to do it than by doing what you enjoy the most. It'll give you the boost you need.

• Sunday 26 March •

Put on your counsellor's hat today. Like it or not, you're the one that friends and family often turn to when the going gets tough and you'll probably be asked to lend a sympathetic ear to a family member who really needs your support today. You may not be able to solve the problem, but you will be able to help them come up with a solution.

• Monday 27 March •

You are blessed with the stamina of a world-class athlete today, and the determination that goes with it. While everyone else is flagging by tea-time, you will be starting to pick up speed! This is just as well because you have a list of chores as long as your arm, and you may also have a deadline to meet. No wonder you often end up working alone – you are still going strong when everyone else has fallen by the wayside.

• *Tuesday 28 March* •

Take care today because a certain person seems determined to pick holes in whatever you do. They may be deliberately trying to undermine you or they could be taking their bad mood out on you. Either way, you won't like being the butt of someone's aggression but what can you do to stop it? One option may be to stick up for yourself, even if you know this will provoke a shouting match.

• *Wednesday 29 March* •

Take care if you're travelling today as there could be some unexpected disruptions to your journey. Allow plenty of extra time and try to adopt a relatively philosophical attitude to any last-minute changes. Fortunately, you're in a fairly relaxed mood and you know how counter-productive it is to get into a state when the situation is beyond your control.

• *Thursday 30 March* •

After all the concerted efforts you've been making recently, this is a good day to take a back seat and let others do all the hard work. Of course, you'll want to be there delegating and making sure that everything gets done, but have you considered how nice it would be to step back for a change? If that sounds like a good idea, why not give it a go?

• *Friday 31 March* •

Matters of the heart are uppermost in your thoughts today. If you're wondering how best to show someone how passionately you feel about them, try some tangible proof of affection rather than simple words. Perhaps you could treat them to a couple of days away, or give them a gift that you know they'd treasure. A small gesture goes a long way now.

APRIL AT A GLANCE

Love	♥ ♥ ♥ ♥ ♥
Money	£ $
Career	💻 💻
Health	☼ ☼ ☼

• *Saturday 1 April* •

If you're about to embark on a major home improvement project, make sure you know you'll be able to finish it. Although you may have great plans for sweeping changes, your enthusiasm could dwindle when the demands of everyday life take over. Perhaps you could start on a less ambitious scale, in the certain knowledge that the job will get done?

• *Sunday 2 April* •

It seems that whenever you try to set aside some time for yourself, someone or something demands your attention and you're forced to give up whatever it is you're doing. You may have to set some very clear boundaries so that you really can ensure some peace and quiet for yourself. Things will only change if you can be direct and say what you need.

• *Monday 3 April* •

Today you are given the opportunity to get to know a neighbour better or to deepen your relationship with a close relative. Either way, you'll benefit enormously from being more open and honest with them. You express yourself with subtlety and delicacy today, and you have a greater ability than usual to establish a rapport. Put all this together and you have the recipe for making everyone happy!

• *Tuesday 4 April* •

During the coming fortnight you will feel extremely single-minded over an issue connected with your home and family, and there will be no point in anyone trying to persuade you to soften your approach. Someone has to take charge of the situation and you will feel that in this case it should be you. Even though you're probably right, you could run the risk of treading on a few people's toes.

• *Wednesday 5 April* •

It's one of those rare days when everything looks crystal clear and you know exactly what to do, especially when it comes to your home or finances. This means that you have the foresight you need to plan ahead and get the ball rolling. Even though you're reconciled to occasional setbacks or delays, you feel ready to take on the world at the moment. Long may it last!

• *Thursday 6 April* •

Allow your partner to make a fuss of you today – you deserve it! Although you tend to believe that it's better to give than to receive, it's important to redress the balance occasionally. It may feel odd at first but you'll be surprised at how quickly you could get used to being pampered. And have you considered how much pleasure it will give your loved one to look after you?

• *Friday 7 April* •

Much as you need a certain amount of structure to your life, for the next few weeks you will be acting more on impulse than auto-pilot. And you will leave no stone unturned in your quest to inject a little more spontaneity into your life. It's not that there aren't a lot of good things already in place, it's simply that you're ready to add a few more.

• Saturday 8 April •

Are you ready to bask in the spotlight? If you are a typical Capricorn you deserve a medal for all your hard work and perseverance, so get ready to take centre stage and enjoy being appreciated and admired. You aren't one to blow your own trumpet, but you're not going to get away with playing down your abilities today. And if you're really honest with yourself, you don't really want to!

• Sunday 9 April •

You can either get an enormous amount done today or you might fritter away your energies and not accomplish anything. You're spoilt for choice and everything is equally appealing, so the trick is to decide what you want to do. Rather than get trapped in a dilemma or switch from one activity to another and then back again, why not pick something at random and just take it from there?

• Monday 10 April •

Do you feel slightly agitated? If you or your partner have been allowing any resentment or anger to build up, you'd better get it out into the open before things turn nasty. Make sure you spend some time together today to allow each of you to say how you're both feeling. This may be enough to defuse the situation and bring you closer together.

• Tuesday 11 April •

Don't worry if your day doesn't go according to plan. What you have in mind and what actually happens will be two very different things, but they could involve a blessing in disguise. You will only experience frustration if you stubbornly set your heart on a particular outcome and refuse to allow anything else to happen. Stay flexible and you could be pleasantly surprised.

• *Wednesday 12 April* •

This is a good day to sort out any queries connected with your finances. Is it time to review the way you handle your money matters? If you need to get advice, make sure you choose someone who has a good reputation and the relevant expertise. When everything is going so well, the last thing you need is to make a bad investment.

• *Thursday 13 April* •

Your thoughts start to turn towards your home and family from today, and you will continue to think about them until the end of the month. During this time you could get involved in some important discussions about the way your home is run, or you might enjoy chatting about the past. Don't be surprised if you feel quite sentimental or nostalgic at times. How about looking through some old keepsakes?

• *Friday 14 April* •

Do you feel like throwing a party? You'll be in your element if you can do some entertaining at home today, and no expense will be spared. You're in the mood to lavish your guests with good food and fine wines as a way of showing them just how much you value their friendship. And if your budget doesn't stretch to anything too grandiose, they'll still appreciate some modest treats.

• *Saturday 15 April* •

Don't take anything at face value today because something that you thought was sorted out now has a question mark hanging over it. Perhaps you were never given the correct information or maybe someone has moved the goalposts. You may need to do some detective work to get to the bottom of this mix-up, so be prepared to roll up your sleeves and do some digging.

• Sunday 16 April •

Trying to keep several balls in the air today may turn out to be far too ambitious. Do you really need to keep yourself quite so busy? Although you will quickly get bored if things become too mundane, it will still do you good to have a breather for a change. However, a family matter or domestic crisis may cause a temporary interruption but things will soon settle down again.

• Monday 17 April •

You could find yourself digging deep into your pockets today when you are asked to donate to a good cause. Alternatively, charity might begin at home, and you could put yourself out in order to help someone or give them a boost. You will enjoy buying items that are just for you and which you don't have to share with anyone else. Even so, your current generosity of spirit may mean that everyone benefits from your spending spree.

• Tuesday 18 April •

The iron hand in the velvet glove is the best way to describe your professional approach during the coming fortnight. You may be smooth-talking but you will certainly mean business, as colleagues and associates are about to find out! It will be a marvellous opportunity to go full steam ahead for your long-term goals, but you will also get the chance to adjust any ambitions that aren't working out in their current form.

• Wednesday 19 April •

Your love life starts to flourish from today, and you can look forward to some great times during the coming month. Don't worry if you are currently a solo Capricorn because Cupid could have you in his sights. Alternatively, you might lose your heart to a creative or artistic enterprise that allows you to explore talents you never knew you had. It will also be a great excuse to celebrate anything you fancy!

• *Thursday 20 April* •

It will be hard to disguise the fact that you're on a short fuse today. Of course, you would find it a lot easier to remain cool, calm and collected if everything was on your terms instead of having to take everyone else's wishes into consideration. However, it's not working out like that. If you really want to avoid a confrontation, you will have to resign yourself to not getting your own way.

• *Friday 21 April* •

You are in a very generous and thoughtful mood today, and some lucky person is going to benefit! You might drop some money into a charity collecting tin or you could decide to go one better than that and help someone close to home. A certain person may want to confide in you or cry on your shoulder, in which case you may be prompted to count your blessings or reflect on your own good fortune.

• *Saturday 22 April* •

You can't quite put your finger on what's bothering you today but you're feeling strangely ill at ease. It could be that something you haven't resolved from the past comes back to haunt you, or you might be bothered about what someone says to you. It may be uncomfortable to get your feelings out into the open but it will be a weight off your mind when you do.

• *Sunday 23 April* •

The air feels a lot clearer today and you're probably breathing a sigh of relief. This is a great day just to have fun and really

enjoy the lighter side of life. You're feeling delightfully carefree and you're ready to try something you've always wanted
to do but could never quite pluck up the courage to tackle
before now. The experience could be positively liberating!

• *Monday 24 April* •

If you need to impress someone today you could make a powerful impact without even trying. All you have to do is be yourself
and your true colours will shine through. And this will be a
wonderful reminder of the fact that you can now reap what
you've sown and put everything that you've learnt to good use.
The view certainly looks good from where you're standing.

• *Tuesday 25 April* •

Get ready to scale new heights as you prepare to embark on a
new endeavour. Whatever your new plan is, it seems a sure-
fire winner as you've already looked at every eventuality and
left nothing to chance. Getting financial support doesn't seem
to be a problem either, as you have more than proved how
capable you really are.

• *Wednesday 26 April* •

Even if you suffer from a moment of self-doubt today, it won't
take you long to get back on track. It's important, however, to
allow yourself to examine any worries that you have because
some of them may be valid. Rather than push them to the
back of your mind, it will be much better in the long run to
acknowledge them. You will feel on safer ground because you
will have identified what needs to be worked on.

• *Thursday 27 April* •

You're not in the happiest of moods today, and in fact you
could be feeling quite low. You have temporarily lost your

enthusiasm and you're probably asking yourself why you bother sometimes. Rather than allow your despondency to colour your whole day, why not seek out a friend who will know exactly how to help you see things in a more positive light?

• *Friday 28 April* •

Sparks could be flying today because the atmosphere between you and a loved one is rather fraught. You've got a pretty good idea of what's at the root of this discord and it really is up to you to offer the olive branch. Putting your feelings into words isn't always easy, but simply hoping that an uncomfortable situation will go away will only make matters worse. Grasp the nettle!

• *Saturday 29 April* •

Whatever your trump card is, now is the time to play it. You've had to make a lot of important decisions recently and not all of them have met with complete approval. However, something you've wanted to discuss for a long time can finally be broached now. And because you feel so strongly convinced and committed to what you believe, people will find you utterly irresistible.

• *Sunday 30 April* •

Go at your own pace today and give yourself time to mull things over. It will do you the world of good to slow down for a while and take things a little easier, even though this may take some getting used to. Allowing yourself to appreciate all the simple pleasures of life that you are sometimes too busy to enjoy isn't too much to ask of yourself, is it?

MAY AT A GLANCE

Love	♥ ♥ ♥ ♥ ♥
Money	£ $
Career	💻 💻 💻 💻 💻
Health	☼ ☼ ☼ ☼ ☼

• *Monday 1 May* •

What a wonderful start to May! There is a definite upswing in your love life from today, and you could be very popular indeed during the next three weeks. A certain person might make it more than obvious that they can't live without you, and you will gain tremendous satisfaction from being around your favourite people. Your social life will also keep you in great demand. Have fun!

• *Tuesday 2 May* •

You could be thrown off balance today by the behaviour of a member of the family. If they've been unpredictable recently and you haven't been able to fathom what's got into them, now is the time to tackle the issue. The direct approach will work better than beating about the bush, but be careful not to be provocative because the situation could be more explosive than you think.

• *Wednesday 3 May* •

The planets are certainly smiling on you at the moment and it looks as though your finances are about to take a turn for the better. If you are in the mood to speculate, your hunches will more than likely pay off between now and mid-June. On the other hand, you could reap enormous benefits from investments that you made in the past. You will also enjoy striking a bargain or doing some tough negotiating.

• *Thursday 4 May* •

Things are definitely looking up! You are feeling much happier than you have been recently and there might even be a rainbow round your shoulder – have you checked? If you have been biting your fingernails about the welfare of a loved one, there could be good news in the pipeline during the coming fortnight. You could also receive an invitation that is a wonderful excuse to get dressed up to the nines. You'll knock everyone's eyes out!

• *Friday 5 May* •

You may well have to put your money where your mouth is today and say exactly what's on your mind. If there's been a situation at work that you've been less than happy about, now is the time to clear the air. It could all boil down to a lack of communication, so make sure you get your point of view across rather than make assumptions about what other people think or want from you.

• *Saturday 6 May* •

How good are you at keeping a deadpan face? You may have to practise today when a certain person's actions threaten to send your eyebrows into orbit. They might buy something that you think is hideous but which they adore, or they could make a suggestion that you think is frankly crazy. However, for various reasons you can't say so and you have to pretend that nothing is wrong. Good luck!

• *Sunday 7 May* •

It's an ideal day to have some fun with your family and loved ones, so how about having a day out together? You can leave your worries on the doorstep and allow yourself to be happy and carefree. If you're a typical Capricorn, you may not often give yourself permission to let go and play, but today you could discover what you've been missing. You might even want to do it more often!

• Monday 8 May •

It will be almost impossible to nail anything or anyone down today, so you might as well give up trying. This is especially likely when it comes to money matters. Frustrating as this may feel at the time, there could be a silver lining to this particular cloud. Be patient and let things unfold at their own pace rather than try to force issues. You'll be amazed at how easy it all is when the time is right for things to happen.

• Tuesday 9 May •

If you're signing any important document today, make sure that everything is completely watertight. A business partner or loved one may not be revealing their true motives and could be pulling the wool over your eyes or not giving you the whole story. It's important that you separate your emotions from the situation so that you can get a true perspective and don't make an error of judgement.

• Wednesday 10 May •

You're still inclined to err on the side of caution today, and with good reason. Giving someone the benefit of the doubt could have serious consequences or mean that you end up kicking yourself. You're far better off double-checking that everything is above board before you take any further action. At least that way you can minimize any potential damage and you will also know what and who you are dealing with.

• *Thursday 11 May* •

You can't decide whether to stick with the devil you know or explore a completely untried path today. You've got a hunch that it may pay off to take a gamble and do something unprecedented, but the prospect of failing at this fills you with dread. Nothing in life is certain, and perhaps you have to allow yourself the odd mistake in order to extend your experience and grow?

• *Friday 12 May* •

If you have been thinking ahead and wondering where to go on your next holiday, now is the time to stock up on travel brochures and do some serious planning. You've probably got your whole itinerary worked out already if you're true to your Sun sign. Unless you're going on your own, however, you may need to consult the other people concerned as not everyone likes to be regimented!

• *Saturday 13 May* •

Everything has been looking pretty rosy for you recently but today you could run into a thicket of thorns. Serious doubts could be raised in your mind about a certain person, and this will give you a lot of pain. You may wonder whether they are as committed to you as they say, or the boot might be on the other foot and you might even be doubting your own emotional commitment. Don't do anything rash – bide your time and see if this crisis blows over.

• *Sunday 14 May* •

How are your energy levels? You will soon get the chance to find out because life is about to keep you really busy. The pace of your working life could increase by leaps and bounds, and you will be leaping about trying to get everything done in time. Will you enjoy this? Yes, because you will love feeling that you've got your finger on the pulse and you will be helped by an ability to think of six things at once. You know how capable you are, and this is your chance to prove it!

• Monday 15 May •

Just because you've always done something in a certain way, it doesn't mean that it's the only way or even the best way. This is an ideal day to discover what the alternatives are and how they could alter your whole approach to everyday tasks. As a result, you could find that your style of working becomes both exciting and innovative. So be prepared to experiment and go out on a limb.

• Tuesday 16 May •

If you are working as part of a team today or coordinating any sort of group activity, make sure you're on the same page as everyone else or everything is likely to take twice as long. You all need to work to one agenda and that should be stated very clearly from the outset if you want to avoid total chaos and confusion.

• Wednesday 17 May •

Put on your dancing shoes because this promises to be one of the highlights of your entire month. It's a fabulous day for going out with someone special, especially if you can do something that you really enjoy or have a wonderful treat. Your feelings for your loved ones know no bounds now, so it's perfect for telling someone how you feel. If you feel shy at the thought of that, make sure that your actions speak louder than words.

• *Thursday 18 May* •

At times over the coming fortnight you could feel like an emotional volcano when powerful feelings within you threaten to erupt. You may have underestimated how strongly you feel about something, and you could be thrown temporarily off balance as a result. The good news is that you will be able to draw on inner reserves so you can regain your equilibrium without denying the intensity of your emotions.

• *Friday 19 May* •

It will be horribly easy to let things get on top of you today, so try not to let that happen. You will be especially susceptible over work and health matters, and you could be tempted to bite your fingernails down to the quick once you start to worry about something. It may seem as though circumstances are beyond your control, in which case perhaps you should alter your attitude if you can't alter the situation?

• *Saturday 20 May* •

If only you could be in two different places at once! Then you would just about manage everything that you have to do today. At least you'll be able to think on your feet and not waste any time. The only thing that's likely to hold you up is dealing with questions from certain people. Make sure you keep them informed and don't go over their heads unless it's absolutely necessary.

• *Sunday 21 May* •

Make this a stress-free day and try to get some fresh air and exercise. You will be able to sort out a lot of mental clutter if you take yourself off for a long walk and let your thoughts unwind. You'll feel a lot more calm and relaxed, and you will then be in a much more positive frame of mind to enjoy the rest of the weekend. Getting out and socializing in the evening could be just what the doctor ordered.

• *Monday 22 May* •

Think big today and your plans will follow suit. All your hard work and efforts are beginning to pay dividends and yet you still have so much that you want to do. If anything, your recent successes have only whetted your appetite to do bigger and better things. You're in that enviable position of being content with yourself and yet you know that it's all still to play for.

• *Tuesday 23 May* •

A loved one could put you on a pedestal today because they have so much admiration for you. Although your ego won't complain too much at such a vote of confidence, ultimately you would probably be more comfortable if this person could see you as a mere mortal, warts and all. At least that way you are allowed to be human and to make mistakes occasionally.

• *Wednesday 24 May* •

Your attention turns to finances today and you're determined to clear any outstanding money matters and wipe the slate clean. Make your intentions clear to the people concerned because then you can negotiate exactly the terms you want. It's also a great day to put forward some revolutionary ideas that are currently exciting you or that will make a big difference to your work situation.

• *Thursday 25 May* •

Keeping your feet on the ground today won't be an easy task. Exciting developments have you buzzing and the wires will be scorching hot as you telegraph the news far and wide. If this unexpected event is connected with work, you can be sure that this is only the beginning and that everything is about to gather momentum in a most stimulating way.

• Friday 26 May •

All is not as it seems today and you may have to make an important decision without being able to weigh up all the facts. Don't jump to conclusions and assume that what you already know is reliable information. Someone could be giving you half truths and you really need to find out what they're up to before you can go any further. Proceed with caution!

• Saturday 27 May •

You've got a clear stretch of open road ahead of you today, with not an obstacle in sight. In fact, whatever you set your sights on will have a much more positive outcome than you can imagine at this stage. So don't limit your thinking but make sure that your goal is attainable and that you can achieve it with relative ease. Why struggle when you don't have to?

• Sunday 28 May •

The home fires burn brightly today as friends, family and familiar surroundings offer you a haven of peace and contentment. Relax and enjoy the love and support that you know you can count on from those who matter most to you. If you haven't been on the best of terms with one family member recently, now is the time to build bridges and patch things up. The results will be truly worthwhile.

• Monday 29 May •

Close relationships are in the spotlight for the next few weeks and you will get the opportunity for a chance encounter or a deeper connection with an existing partner. You could even experience a telepathic bond with them, making you realize how aware you are of your loved one's needs. It will also be a marvellous chance to talk about how you feel or to discuss any difficulties between you.

• *Tuesday 30 May* •

You may come across someone today who's in need of your sympathy and support. This won't require a great effort on your part because you will know exactly how to respond to the situation. Even if you've never given advice before, you will intuitively know what to say and will offer not only practical help but a few words of wisdom as well.

• *Wednesday 31 May* •

It's one of those irritating days when you feel you are taking one step forwards and two steps back. Someone could be dragging their heels over something or using subtle tactics to express their displeasure with you. It will be easy to allow yourself to be sucked in to the other person's games and to be undermined as a result. A loved one may also be feeling sorry for themselves, but do you agree with their analysis of the situation?

JUNE AT A GLANCE

Love	❤ ❤ ❤ ❤ ❤
Money	£ $
Career	💻 💻 💻 💻 💻
Health	☼ ☼ ☼ ☼ ☼

• *Thursday 1 June* •

You are full of confidence today, especially when it comes to making your mark on the world. You could have some very good ideas about ways to improve your working situation or you could see exactly where a colleague is going wrong and what they should do to put things right. However, your comments may not go down very well because people may be very resistant to the idea of change. Wait a while and then try again.

• *Friday 2 June* •

If you've had any health concerns recently today's New Moon is suggesting that you seek medical advice and then do whatever is necessary to get yourself back in top form. Even if you feel in the pink at the moment, this is a great opportunity to consider how well you look after yourself and how big a priority your health is. If you always take your body for granted, perhaps it's about time you started to take more care of yourself? Who knows, you might even enjoy it!

• *Saturday 3 June* •

Your thinking is lightning quick today, and if you add this to your single-mindedness you could make considerable headway on any current projects. You've got lots of new ideas and the energy and stamina to take them beyond the planning stage. The only fly in the ointment could be your impatience at waiting for everyone else to come up to speed. Don't rush them into things before they are ready to accept them.

• Sunday 4 June •

This is a good day to share your feelings with a loved one and to create a stronger bond between the two of you. There's a mutual receptivity between you which makes you both very open to each other. If one of you has a grievance to air, what better time than now to resolve any unspoken resentment and deepen your rapport?

• Monday 5 June •

Something that has been preoccupying you could come to light today. The problem is that you now have to confront either a partner or associate with what you have finally uncovered. Diplomacy won't really work in this situation – you may need to be far more up-front with the truth. You could be accused of being arrogant, but at least you'll have taken charge of the situation.

• Tuesday 6 June •

If you need to win the confidence or cooperation of a work-mate, this is a great day to do it. Other people are very receptive to you today and they will happily listen to you. What's more, you have no wish to ram your ideas down anyone's throat and are quite content to say your piece and then let others make up their own minds. There could also be some good news about some money that is owed to you.

• Wednesday 7 June •

You might badly over-estimate your abilities today and end up making a fool of yourself, so be careful. Try to be as realistic as possible, especially where your own limits are concerned.

Better to clip your wings now rather than fly too high and set yourself up for a fall. It may cost you in the short term to lower your expectations, but this tactic will pay off in the long run.

• *Thursday 8 June* •

See today as an experience that will equip you brilliantly for whatever it is you're endeavouring to do. Your mind is like a sponge and you can assimilate a lot of information in a short space of time. All this can be done with relative ease, which makes the whole process effortless and stimulating. And you'll enjoy it so much you won't even feel overloaded!

• *Friday 9 June* •

Pay attention to detail today and make sure that all the Ts are crossed and the Is dotted. You need to deal with certain practicalities, which involves keeping a close eye on the fine print. If you're making any verbal agreements with someone, double-check that you've both got a clear understanding of what you're undertaking. Otherwise, there could be trouble further down the line.

• *Saturday 10 June* •

There are times when placating others is not in your own best interests, but this is one of those days when you have nothing to lose by it. Accommodating the wishes of other people isn't any skin off your nose today and it will still allow you to get on with what you need to do. It's one of those rare occasions when everyone can do exactly what they choose and, far from creating resentment, an air of harmony prevails.

• *Sunday 11 June* •

This may be the day of rest but that's the last thin~ like doing. Do you really need to keep so bu~

your day with unnecessary activities, be selective about how you use your time and you'll feel a much greater sense of satisfaction. Not only that, you'll also have energy in reserve which will give you a head start for the week ahead.

● Monday 12 June ●

Something that you've been planning proves to be elusive today and it looks as though it may not materialize after all. As disappointed as you are, a part of you is also secretly relieved. What you may now realize is that you were going along with the general consensus, when deep down you weren't as wholehearted as everyone else. Perhaps it's time to focus on what you truly believe in.

● Tuesday 13 June ●

You can cut a swathe through any obstacle today, armed with nothing more than a few kind words and a sympathetic ear. Partners respond especially well to your more gentle approach but everyone will be far more responsive and willing to cooperate than usual. It's not that you can't be forceful if necessary, it's simply that it's not needed in this situation.

● Wednesday 14 June ●

Decision, decisions! If there's an invitation to go out tonight you're probably in two minds about it. Do you let your hair down and pay the price the next morning or do you decide to stay at home and have an early night? The reason it feels like a dilemma at all is probably because you're feeling physically under par today and you need to pace yourself.

● Thursday 15 June ●

You can recharge your batteries and replenish your reserves today. If you're a typical Capricorn, you normally have energy in reserve and it doesn't take long to top up your levels of stamina. Avoid the temptation to take on too much and instead do things that you know you enjoy and which energize you. Before you know it, you'll be back to normal.

• *Friday 16 June* •

Today's Full Moon may create some stress in your everyday life over the next two weeks, particularly at work. Something in you has reached boiling point and it may be hard to control your anger or frustration. A confrontation of some sort may be inevitable and could even resolve some old resentments that have remained unspoken for far too long. Once the dust has settled, you will be glad that the situation has been sorted out.

• *Saturday 17 June* •

It's one of those days when you are filled with a sense of urgency and a need to get things done. Rather than rush around in circles, trying to do three things at once and ending up wearing yourself out, it will be far more productive to write a list of all the chores that you want to tackle and then work your way through them systematically. If you start to feel frustrated or angry, do something therapeutic, otherwise you could become accident-prone.

• *Sunday 18 June* •

It's a question of give and take over the next few weeks when you realize that the only way to sort things out is to compromise. If you're being honest with yourself, you'll recognize that it really isn't any great hardship to meet someone halfway and actually it creates far more balance in any partnership. Perhaps you can now fight for the relationship as opposed to fighting about it.

• Monday 19 June •

An air of peace and cooperation prevails today and you have good reason to feel pleased about the amount of hard work you've put in to attain this. Everything seems to flow and all your dealings with others run smoothly and effortlessly. If only life were always like this! Try to find time to do something enjoyable with a special person. Even a mini treat will buck you up.

• Tuesday 20 June •

Capricorns aren't exactly renowned for their complacency but today you really are feeling content with yourself. You're a joy to be with and you'll draw people to you even if they have kept their distance in the past. That is because you're far more approachable when you're in this frame of mind. Lowering your guard has all sorts of benefits, as you are now finding out.

• Wednesday 21 June •

There are times when it is best to go it alone and there are times, such as the coming four weeks, when it is far more beneficial to surround yourself with other people. Any form of teamwork will be very productive, and you may even feel that you function best when you are part of a partnership. Relationships of all kinds will be constructive now, whether they are platonic, romantic or professional.

• Thursday 22 June •

Whether you choose to immerse yourself in a team project or join in the social whirl today, you need to prove to yourself that you belong. Integrating and involving yourself more with those around you has become a priority and, fortunately, you can now feel much more secure about your place in the scheme of things. Feeling more comfortable in yourself will mean that other people are much more willing to accept you as you are.

• *Friday 23 June* •

Are you feeling absent-minded? Things may go missing today or you could lose something altogether. At least you can try to minimize the likelihood of this happening before you go out by making sure that anything essential stays close at hand. If something does go astray and you can't remember where you put it, don't be in a hurry to find it as it may take a couple of weeks before it shows up again.

• *Saturday 24 June* •

Love and romance are well-starred today and the chemistry between you and a loved one is particularly potent. You could be about to discover untapped feelings and desires that are ready to run rampant and bring a sense of excitement to your current relationship. Being spontaneous is terrific fun now and you might decide that you are going to behave like this more often in future.

• *Sunday 25 June* •

You're in a very assertive mood today and in no doubt at all about what you need. Most importantly, you aren't embarrassed about the way you feel or shy about voicing these feelings. Being so forthright emotionally may not be your normal behaviour but, when the situation requires it, you are able to pull out all the stops and put your inhibitions to the back of your mind.

• *Monday 26 June* •

You are being given the go-ahead today to take charge of a domestic situation. You're in the unique position of being able to clear the air rather than muddy the waters, and this is exactly what is required. Being able to stand back from the problem so that you can see it clearly will help you to work out the best strategy. It will also ensure that you don't get het up if things threaten to become tricky.

• Tuesday 27 June •

It's one of those days when you want to enjoy yourself whenever you get the chance, so what have you got planned? Ideally, you should take the day off and do something that you really enjoy, especially if you can take a certain person along for the ride. Even if that isn't possible, there is no need to miss out completely. Arrange to do something after you have finished work or invite someone round to your place.

• Wednesday 28 June •

You are in quite a serious mood today, especially when it comes to your love life. Although you aren't in any danger of being unduly pessimistic or gloomy about your relationship with you-know-who, you are viewing it in a very realistic and sensible light. Your concern for one special person is more than obvious, and you may have to find a balance between letting them go their own sweet way and keeping a solicitous eye on them.

• Thursday 29 June •

A wonderful feeling of happiness and well-being steals over you today. You're surrounded by people who bring out the best in you and who you know have your best interests at heart. No wonder you're feeling on top of the world! It's the perfect day for going to a celebration or getting all dolled up for a social event. You are determined to enjoy yourself to the hilt, and that is exactly what you will do!

• *Friday 30 June* •

If you have been feeling fed up about your work prospects or you've been dragging yourself around, feeling like a wet lettuce, help is now at hand. During the next few months you will get the chance to turn situations to your advantage and to seize some fabulous opportunities to improve your health or working life. Don't be afraid to take chances or to have faith in your abilities, because the results could be brilliant.

JULY AT A GLANCE

Love	♥ ♥ ♥ ♥ ♥
Money	£ $ £
Career	🖥 🖥
Health	☼ ☼

• *Saturday 1 July* •

Today's New Moon makes it an energetic start to the month, and it is especially reassuring where your relationships are concerned. During the coming fortnight you will get the chance to grow closer to a certain person, particularly if you can let down your emotional guard and be honest with yourself about how you feel. This is also the perfect time to get a new alliance off the ground, particularly if it involves making a commitment to one another.

• *Sunday 2 July* •

You don't need to go far afield to enjoy yourself today as you'll be your happiest on home ground with family and loved ones. Although you are very aware of your commitments and sense of responsibility to those you care about, you have also learnt to value your independence and freedom more. Have you noticed how much better you feel as a result?

• *Monday 3 July* •

Someone may be trying to keep you from seeing the whole picture today, making you suspect that they have a hidden agenda. Rather than respond in kind to their cloak and dagger behaviour, you are more likely to disarm them by being totally honest and open. Once you've said your piece and shown yourself in your true light, you'll then have to decide if you still want this person in your life.

• *Tuesday 4 July* •

Yesterday's contretemps has probably unsettled you and left you feeling out of sorts. If so, perhaps you should congratulate yourself on your ability to handle a difficult situation? Take care in all financial matters because you could easily feel guilty about spending too much money recently or you might be wondering if you can afford to do something that seems rather extravagant or self-indulgent. Don't be too hard on yourself!

• *Wednesday 5 July* •

Slow down! You could put yourself under a lot of pressure today, thinking about that list of things you've got to do and wondering how on earth you're going to get it all done. One task in particular may be even be keeping you awake at night, and the more you think about it the more daunting it becomes. Rather than tie yourself in knots, it will be far more productive to take a deep breath and then do the very thing that you feel so worried about. The relief will be tremendous.

• *Thursday 6 July* •

Be warned that you may not get much done today. That's because everyone seems to be in a very chatty mood and they could keep interrupting you. The phone may ring more than usual or someone could drop round unexpectedly. Talking to other people will help you to marshal your thoughts and it might also give you the chance to discuss ideas that are currently simmering in your mind.

• *Friday 7 July* •

It was easy to talk to people yesterday but things aren't quite the same today. Someone might be so outspoken or direct that you feel shaken by what they have to say. They won't pull their punches but are they right in what they tell you? Be prepared for some raised voices or tricky moments, especially if one of you has been feeling angry for some time but is only now starting to admit it.

• *Saturday 8 July* •

Much as you'd like to spend time romancing your loved one today you still have a few work-related matters to deal with. This could prove to be a source of conflict and the only way to resolve it is for you to decide what's more important. Try to see this from your partner's point of view, as well as your own. Isn't there some kind of compromise that you can reach?

• *Sunday 9 July* •

If the plaster is still falling from the ceiling after yesterday's little dust-up, you may be feeling rather emotionally fragile today. Even though there may be things that you feel you need to get off your chest, once that is done it is time to kiss and make up. Go on, bury the hatchet and do something enjoyable together!

• *Monday 10 July* •

Your bark may be worse than your bite but you are certainly a force to be reckoned with today. Whatever the circumstances, a display of strength on your part will unequivocally establish your authority and give you the edge on everyone else. Make sure that you keep the channels of communication open so that you can reach an understanding if that is what's needed.

• *Tuesday 11 July* •

You are digging your heels in today over an intensely personal matter and it looks as though you could reach an impasse unless somebody decides to relent. If you're true to your Sun sign you will stick to your principles because you're unlikely to change the habit of a lifetime now. You have absolutely no doubt in your mind that being dogged and determined in this situation is the only way to behave. What makes you so sure?

• *Wednesday 12 July* •

There have been some tense moments during the past few days but you are now ready and willing to put them behind you. In fact, you're in such a sunny mood that you are only interested in enjoying yourself. Choose a form of entertainment that really lifts your spirits and brings a smile to your face. And if your sense of humour has gone AWOL recently, now's the time to find it.

• *Thursday 13 July* •

You could be feeling in an extravagant mood over the next few weeks and ready to pamper yourself. Treating yourself to something new or spending some money on an item that you've always wanted to own will do you the power of good. If you're the sort of Capricorn who feels guilty about being a little self-indulgent, now is the time to recognize how beneficial it is to spoil yourself every now and then.

• *Friday 14 July* •

Take care today because you could easily feel as though you have been cast adrift from your emotional moorings. Someone might hurt you badly or you could spend a lot of time brooding about things that may never happen. Although you should avoid ruminating on your worries, you will nevertheless be much happier if you are left to your own devices. Trying to be sociable when you are feeling solitary will only make you feel worse.

• *Saturday 15 July* •

If you've got something to celebrate today you're likely to do it in style. You may even want to throw caution to the winds and spend lots of money in the cause of having fun. Whatever the reason for your current buoyancy and optimism, it's likely to prove contagious so there'll be no shortage of company to share the occasion. You may even be trampled in the rush!

• *Sunday 16 July* •

Today's Full Moon means that any current relationship difficulties could reach a climax during the next two weeks. The balance between your personal and professional life is probably at the root of the tension and redressing this has now become an urgent priority. It may be more challenging than you think to return to the status quo. Wait until you're thinking straight again before you attempt to patch things up.

• *Monday 17 July* •

It hasn't always been easy to put across your point of view recently. Other people may have misunderstood what you are trying to say or you could have sent out mixed signals. Thank goodness all that changes from today, when communications start to return to normal. Not only will you find it easier to say what you think, partners will also be much more approachable and receptive.

• *Tuesday 18 July* •

If you're footloose and fancy free you could be swept off your feet today by a seductive stranger. Although this may be a beautiful romantic experience, it may not last for very long. If you're looking for someone reliable and committed, this person may not come up to scratch. Even if you are part of a happy couple, you could be sorely tempted by someone's charms today.

• *Wednesday 19 July* •

You can afford to take the running of your everyday life for granted today and concentrate on helping a close relative or casual acquaintance. This isn't the first time you've had to step into the breach but at least it gives you the upper hand in the decision-making process. As long as you don't lose your objectivity, you can get matters sorted out both efficiently and diplomatically.

• *Thursday 20 July* •

Your energy levels are high and you're in a very positive frame of mind today. You feel more confident and enthusiastic than usual and you want to try something new. If you decide to embark on a new project, just one word of caution is needed. Make sure that this isn't a flash in the pan and that you can actually sustain an interest beyond the initial stages.

• *Friday 21 July* •

If you think carefully you will be able to gain some very useful insights into the things that matter to you at the moment. One very special relationship in particular will benefit from the deeper understanding you now have of your inner emotional state. This will enable you to relate to each other with greater sensitivity and intensity, not to mention fan the flames of your desire!

• *Saturday 22 July* •

If you are a typical Capricorn you have a strong sense of duty and a real need to be respected by other people. There have been times this year when your efforts have apparently counted for nothing, but all that is about to change. During the coming four weeks you will be in the spotlight and all your hard work will receive the recognition it so richly deserves. This could be anything from a pat on the back to promotion or a new job. Your self-esteem will also rise by leaps and bounds.

• *Sunday 23 July* •

Take care because it's one of those combustible days when all sorts of things have the potential to annoy you. You could lose your temper with a member of the family or a partner, especially if they seem slow on the uptake or they aren't going along with your ideas. Although you may be justified in getting angry, there may be a chance that you are overreacting or using one problem as an outlet for your anger about something else.

• *Monday 24 July* •

Hold on to your hat because it is another day when it's easy to lose your temper and get involved in a big shouting match. Problems connected with joint finances and loved ones will be the no-go areas today. You may think you have a genuine grievance, but do you? Are you making a big to-do about current tensions or are you well within your rights to jump up and down about what is happening?

• *Tuesday 25 July* •

You get the chance to repair any damage from yesterday's outbursts, but you will have to choose your words carefully. The last thing you want is an action replay! You may have to be prepared to eat humble pie in the general interests of everyone concerned, or perhaps you simply haven't the energy to get involved in another round of verbal fisticuffs. Work off any remaining tension by doing something therapeutic.

• *Wednesday 26 July* •

Thank goodness you are feeling much more tolerant today and less bothered by all the recent upsets. You don't feel like making a major drama out of anything and, even if something does go wrong, you will realize that you have the time to solve the problem. What you will most benefit from today is being with good friends and simply enjoying their company.

• *Thursday 27 July* •

Your life feels much more rewarding today and one heartening realization is that you can now build on all good friendships and relationships. You're aware of how fortunate you are, and if you would like to show your appreciation for all the support and love you've received, this is an ideal day to get started. Why not do some entertaining or buy someone a present to say thank you?

• *Friday 28 July* •

Rather than be busy just for the sake of it, make sure you have some quiet time to yourself today so you can mull things over. It's not that you need to do any serious thinking, it's more a case of simply reflecting on how you're feeling about your life in general. You might come up with some interesting revelations that will help you to see certain things in a new light.

• *Saturday 29 July* •

The shops exude a magnetic attraction for you today, but you need to go carefully unless you are feeling very rich indeed. That is because it will be tempting to make free with your credit cards and chequebook, whether you can afford to or not. Impulse buys will be good fun at the time but later on you might wonder what on earth possessed you to choose them. You had better keep the receipts in case you need to take anything back!

• *Sunday 30 July* •

You may be tempted to while away the day in a daydream, and why not! Do whatever it is that most inspires you and you'll feel really replenished for it. You'll be just as happy if you spend the time alone or with someone special. What you really long for now is to be free to do whatever takes your fancy, however much of a whim it may seem to others.

• *Monday 31 July* •

Keep your guard up today as someone in a powerful position may try to persuade you to do something that in your heart you don't believe in. Going against your beliefs is likely to land you in confusion at best and trouble at worst, so think very carefully about how to handle this situation. You wield more influence than you give yourself credit for, so don't be swayed by pressure from outside forces.

AUGUST AT A GLANCE

Love	♥ ♥ ♥ ♥ ♥
Money	£ $ £ $ £
Career	💻 💻 💻 💻
Health	☼ ☼

• *Tuesday 1 August* •

A dispute over a joint property or possessions is almost inevitable during the next few weeks, so go carefully. The resulting conflict could force you re-examine and modify your position. The problem may well lie in a disagreement over the way some joint resources are managed, with the other person adamantly sticking to their point of view and refusing to budge. It will be up to you to break the deadlock.

• *Wednesday 2 August* •

You could be acting quite compulsively today without being aware of how your behaviour is affecting others. You're feeling strongly emotional, which makes it virtually impossible to rationalize the state you're in. Even if you don't like what you hear, you may have to rely on someone close to you to give you some honest feedback.

• *Thursday 3 August* •

Although you have now managed to get your emotions under control, you may still be reeling from yesterday's home truths. Nevertheless, it's a great day to concentrate on creative and artistic ventures because there is a lot that you want to get on with, and you will enjoy channelling your energies into something so productive. You could receive a heartening invitation.

• Friday 4 August •

Once you have set yourself a task you usually do your best to accomplish it – and today's no exception. Your main objective is to reorganize the working pattern of your life so that you can be more in control. However, do make sure that you don't become so focused on this project that you lose track of everything else. Keep a sense of proportion!

• Saturday 5 August •

Provided you don't expect to love everything you do today, you'll be pleasantly surprised when there are some enjoyable moments. At worst, you may find yourself making a compromise with someone so that you wish you had been more honest and said how you felt. At best, you will be able to clear a path for a whole new level of communication between you and your partner, which gives you both a lot more room to manoeuvre.

• Sunday 6 August •

You're ready for a new experience during the next few weeks which will be good fun and will also make you view life in a new way. You might go to a concert and listen to music that is completely different from anything you've heard before, or you could travel to an exotic country which completely captivates you. Whatever happens, this will be a highly enjoyable and thought-provoking time.

• Monday 7 August •

Something you haven't been able to understand about yourself is finally coming to light, much to your relief. You will become increasingly aware of it over the next two weeks. Other people have known this part of you for a long time but, because it's your blind spot, you are the last one to find out about it. You'll be amazed at how this new self-awareness will improve many areas of your life, and especially the way you express yourself.

• *Tuesday 8 August* •

You will feel as though a weight has lifted from you today. There may be certain aspects of your past which you can look at more dispassionately now and feel ready to let go of. You can see very clearly the things that have been holding you back and you no longer feel so bound by them. This will be wonderfully liberating and it will certainly give you more emotional and physical energy.

• *Wednesday 9 August* •

Be very careful today when handling anything connected with finance or possessions because things won't always be quite what they seem. Someone may appear to be scrupulously honest while all the time they are operating some sort of scam or get-rich-quick scheme, or you may find that no one will give you the answers to certain pertinent questions. If in doubt, do nothing until you feel confident that you are better informed about what is going on.

• *Thursday 10 August* •

You embark on a very industrious phase from today, which will have a very positive effect on your working life over the next few months. However, watch out for possible mental overload at times because you will always try to do the very best you possibly can, even if it means working round the clock or foregoing your social life. It will be easy to wear yourself out so it will be even more important than usual to take good care of your health.

• *Friday 11 August* •

Lots of surprising events will keep you on your toes today. Expect the unexpected because anything can and will happen, especially if it is completely different from your usual Friday routine. In a business or professional partnership, you may suddenly have to revise your original plan because of some totally unexpected development. Be prepared to think on your feet and go with the flow, and then all will be well. You might even feel quite excited by developments!

• *Saturday 12 August* •

Are you ready for a night out on the town? Let your hair down today and really enjoy yourself. You're in a fun-loving mood and you need to be with friends who can help you to make the most of it! Your vibrant energy is making you very magnetic, which means you are very attractive to certain people right now. All this adds up to good news if you're looking for romance.

• *Sunday 13 August* •

Someone may come to you today to request a loan or to borrow something of yours that you highly value. It will probably turn out to be their lucky day as you're feeling very generous and benevolent towards them and only too willing to help. What's important to you right now is the well-being of those close to you and how best you can support them.

• *Monday 14 August* •

The jury is out on one particular issue and you may have to wait a while before you get a definitive answer. It doesn't matter how clear and logical the situation might appear to you, the fact is that it's a lot more complex than meets the eye. So resist the temptation to rush to an immediate judgement and allow the truth to come out in its own good time.

• *Tuesday 15 August* •

Today's Full Moon is reminding you that it's about time you had a good think about your long-term hopes and wishes. Is everything still on track or have you taken a few detours and ended up in a dead end? If you strongly suspect that certain dreams are no more than pie in the sky, perhaps it's time to abandon them. However, don't jettison anything that is still a possibility even if it seems remote, or which has enormous emotional significance for you.

• *Wednesday 16 August* •

This isn't a good day to get a balanced perspective on private or very personal problems as you're more likely to be thinking subjectively. You may have the best of intentions about being fair and impartial but they are being coloured by your personal considerations in this matter. You may need an expert opinion to help unravel this confusion and straighten things out. If that doesn't appeal, at least wait a few days before doing anything decisive.

• *Thursday 17 August* •

If you've just heard some news that has disheartened you, try not to think the worst because this will only make you feel more miserable than ever. Wait until tomorrow when your mood has passed and you can decide then how to proceed. In fact, you are more than able to tackle the problem and you will feel a whole lot better when you do. In the meantime, sit tight and don't brood.

• *Friday 18 August* •

You need some peace and quiet today and a place you can retreat to where you can't be disturbed. It's surprising how quickly you can build up your stamina again when you give yourself a proper break. Often Capricorns like their own company and this is a perfect day to have some time to yourself and simply enjoy being on your ownsome. All too soon the world will be knocking at your door again!

• *Saturday 19 August* •

You can make a lot of very positive and far-reaching changes today simply by putting your mind to it. Think about how much power you wield when you want to make an impact and how this can enhance your effectiveness. You're in no doubt about the sort of reforms you want to make in your life, and you're undaunted by the sustained effort this will require. Watch out, world!

• *Sunday 20 August* •

Are you ready for a life-changing encounter? Any new relationship that starts today could have a wonderfully beneficial influence on your attitude to life and create important consequences for your future. It's not every day that you meet someone who has such a profound effect on you, but there's no doubt you're ready for this particular meeting. You may even suspect that destiny has taken a hand!

• *Monday 21 August* •

Don't even try to hide your feelings for a certain person because you'll find it virtually impossible. Love is in the air and you're taking very big breaths! It will be more than obvious to everyone else that you're somewhat intoxicated and they're all dying for you to spill the beans. However hard you try, you won't be able to contain yourself, so they won't be in suspense for long!

• *Tuesday 22 August* •

You've had so many new experiences in the last few days that it's no wonder you don't know whether you're coming or going. Nevertheless, you'd be the last to complain. In fact, you're taking great delight in having your world opened up in such a colourful way. If the opportunity comes up for a holiday abroad, this will only add to your journey of discovery and give you something else to feel good about.

• *Wednesday 23 August* •

You can broaden your horizons even further today, and what better way to do that than to travel. Playing it safe is definitely not what you're interested in at the moment. If you're going to take off it needs to be an exciting adventure which gives you a new and much broader perspective on life. Even if you stay closer to home, you should still fasten your safety belt and prepare yourself for the unknown.

• *Thursday 24 August* •

You are totally engrossed in your own experiences today and very aware of how you're being affected by what's going on around you. If you find yourself in a new environment, you'll have a great desire to discover more about the people you meet and you'll be eager to strike up conversations and discussions with them. Rarely have you been so keen to make the most of life.

• *Friday 25 August* •

The tempo of your social activities is accelerating and your feet will hardly touch the ground today. You're at your most chatty and communicative and you share a lot of common ground with the people you're mixing with. And it's not only the people you meet that you want to connect with, you may also feel inspired to write letters to far-off friends and relatives that you really care about.

• Saturday 26 August •

It won't take much to make you happy today. Wherever you happen to be, you have a strong urge to be in beautiful surroundings in which you can feel relaxed and content. If nowhere comes to mind, ask a loved one if they have a special place that they would love to visit and then head off in that direction. It's a very simple recipe for a wonderful day.

• Sunday 27 August •

Go carefully today because someone or something could really get under your skin. You may find it impossible to think about anything else, which will be highly irritating if it's something that you would rather forget all about. A philosophy or moral code could nag away at you, especially if you feel that you aren't living up to it. Rather than give yourself a hard time when you are already feeling vulnerable, it will be better to distract yourself completely and do something therapeutic.

• Monday 28 August •

More haste, less speed today. You could act in a very rash or impetuous way, which feels great at the time but could land you in hot water once you have simmered down. This is especially likely if you are trying to sort out a joint financial matter or something connected with a very private or sensitive issue. Try to exercise some self-restraint rather than jumping in with both feet.

• Tuesday 29 August •

Are you thinking about starting a new course of study? You've been able to get some of your current restlessness out of your system but you're still looking for something to stretch and inspire you. If there's a subject that you've always wanted to learn but never had the time for, why not sign up for it during the coming fortnight? You've got nothing to lose and a whole lot to gain.

• *Wednesday 30 August* •

If your relationship with a boss or authority figure has been rather dicey recently, over the next few weeks you will get the chance to put things on a more even footing. This may involve soothing a few ruffled feathers and, in extreme cases, it may even mean that you have to butter someone up or massage their ego. However, if that is what it takes to restore the peace or get into someone's good books, perhaps it will be worth it.

• *Thursday 31 August* •

You are blessed with the happy knack of manipulating situations to your advantage today, especially in your professional life. You're not remotely intimidated by people in more powerful positions than you, and in fact you feel extremely confident and at ease with them. Use this keen sense of your own self-worth to secure something that you've been aspiring towards. It's yours for the asking.

SEPTEMBER AT A GLANCE

Love	♥ ♥
Money	£ $
Career	💻 💻 💻 💻 💻
Health	☼ ☼

• *Friday 1 September* •

You will get a chance to show what you're really made of today and you're not likely to disappoint. You're ready to prove to yourself and to others exactly how resourceful and self-reliant you are, and how these skills can be put to even better use than they are at present. Having the measure of your own worth is the key to furthering your ambitions.

• *Saturday 2 September* •

You're about to discover the meaning to the expression 'every cloud has a silver lining'. Even if you meet a challenge today, you'll rise to the occasion and defend yourself in such a way that you'll earn respect – even if others don't agree with you. With hindsight, you'll realize that all of this is only serving to make you stronger and more confident.

• *Sunday 3 September* •

Someone could offer you an intriguing proposal today that may threaten to throw you off-balance. Part of you may want to reject it out of hand because of the commitment it entails, but another part of you is curious and wants to know more. You won't know whether to go for it or not until you've looked at the small print in detail. Make sure you do, in case there are any hidden snags.

• *Monday 4 September* •

Look after yourself today because you could be feeling under the weather and particularly low on energy. It's not surprising – life has been pretty hectic recently and you've been running on empty for a while now. Slow down and make a conscious effort to take it easy until you feel better. Your body isn't a machine so give it some TLC and have a breather for once.

• *Tuesday 5 September* •

If you're keen to take better care of yourself, you could be feeling slightly the worse for wear today. You'd think it would be the other way around, but it takes time to feel the benefit of a new regime. All your accumulated tension and tiredness is starting to come out and that's the reason for feeling under par. Don't worry, you'll soon pick up.

• *Wednesday 6 September* •

Some people really do see you as the fount of all wisdom, and one particular person is likely to be knocking on your door today asking for help. You'll have a choice about whether you tell them what they want to hear, or whether you speak your mind and say what you really feel. They may not like your honest opinion at first, but they'll more than likely thank you in the end.

• *Thursday 7 September* •

You are in a very ambitious state at the moment, and over the next few weeks you will get the chance to think deeply about what you want to do next. You may already have your strategy mapped out or you might still be in the dark about how to realize some of your ambitions. It will be a marvellous time to pick someone's brains or enjoy the benefit of their advice and experience. And don't be surprised if you dispense some advice yourself!

• *Friday 8 September* •

This is a good day to pool your resources with people that you share a common goal with. If you try to make headway alone, you're more likely to come up against irritating logistical problems which will only deflect you from your purpose. It's a good idea to keep everyone in the picture so that you can all pull together to maximum effect.

• *Saturday 9 September* •

This is one of those magical days that you wish would last forever. It's almost as if you're sprinkling fairy dust in all directions, because everything you touch turns to gold. Everyone seems favourably disposed towards you and one of your wishes may come true without you even having to do anything. Life is rich in many ways at the moment, so savour such good fortune while it lasts.

• *Sunday 10 September* •

Make the most of your imagination today because it could take you on some wonderful journeys. You could be inspired about a work project or you might instinctively say the right thing to the right person at the right time, with some very beneficial results. You might also come up with some great ideas about making your money go further, especially if these schemes seem to materialize out of thin air.

• *Monday 11 September* •

Someone could be spoiling for a fight but think twice before you get into an argument with them, especially if you feel that you've been sucked in to their bad mood. You won't do yourself any favours by rising to the bait, and you may even run the risk of blotting your copybook. By simply letting things be, you'll find that the atmosphere returns to normal much quicker than you might have imagined.

• *Tuesday 12 September* •

If you have papered over the cracks in an emotional issue recently, today's events will make you realize that you haven't fooled anyone. The cracks are still there, and they may even be wider than they were before. Rather than burying your head in the sand again, it will be better to bite the bullet and face up to reality. This isn't something you're looking forward to, to say the least, but you know that you don't have much choice.

• *Wednesday 13 September* •

How do you feel about your neighbourhood? Do certain things annoy you and have you been promising yourself to take action for ages? If so, the coming fortnight is the ideal opportunity to finally do something positive. This might involve having a quiet word with a troublesome neighbour, getting involved in a scheme to improve your local environment or anything else that will make your own backyard a happier place.

• *Thursday 14 September* •

You can forget your usual routine because it flies straight out of the window today. The good news is that you'll actually thrive on the change of pace. If you have to work, you'll be looking for as much stimulus as possible to sustain your interest. If you don't have any jobs to do, why not do something entertaining that you wouldn't normally have time to enjoy? Remember that a change is as good as a rest.

• *Friday 15 September* •

Look before you leap today, otherwise you might find yourself in a compromising situation. You could make a chance remark about someone without really knowing anything about them and land yourself in real trouble. Your best bet is to be as diplomatic and tactful as possible, especially when meeting new people. That way, you're less likely to put your foot in it.

• *Saturday 16 September* •

Although you're still feeling outspoken today, you're far less likely to cause offence. Quite the reverse, in fact. Somehow your opinions, however direct and forceful they may seem, will be listened to and respected. The difference is that this time, rather than being flippant, you're taking a much more serious attitude to what you want to say.

• *Sunday 17 September* •

Take it easy between now and early November, and don't push yourself too hard. Everything needs to be approached slowly and carefully if you want your plans to succeed. Trying to accomplish too much in too short a space of time will only frustrate you and make you feel inadequate to the task in hand. It will be better to accept your limitations and eat humble pie than make a fool of yourself.

• *Monday 18 September* •

A certain friendship will really come up trumps today and give your faith in life exactly the boost it needed. This person might put in a good word for you with the powers-that-be, so that people have greater confidence in you and your abilities. Not only that, your popularity rating goes up considerably, making you undeniably flavour of the month!

• *Tuesday 19 September* •

You feel at peace with the world today and confident that everything will turn out all right. Your self-confidence and sense of well-being are so strong that you can rise above any petty irritations that you experience and even tolerate other people's bad moods. In short, you're not prepared to allow any negativity to come between you and your happiness.

• *Wednesday 20 September* •

You receive a tremendous burst of energy today which you need to put to good use. It will be great for rolling up your sleeves and getting on with a lot of hard work, and it's also good for sorting out a financial matter that's become tied up in knots recently. There could also be a few surprises on the agenda, so don't expect everything to happen in the way it was planned.

• *Thursday 21 September* •

Whoops! It's one of those days when you feel you have to tiptoe around on eggshells to avoid annoying someone or earning the sharp edge of their tongue. However, is this such a good idea? If you have felt trouble brewing for some time between you and this person, this is a good opportunity to have it out with them. All the same, ignore the temptation to dredge up past grievances or things that aren't relevant to the current problem.

• *Friday 22 September* •

Check that all your paperwork is up to date today because you might discover that there are some unattended bills or unfinished documents lurking in a drawer. An oversight right now could trip you up just when you're picking up speed. So even though you might resent having to slow down temporarily to check things over, in the long run taking these precautions will save you a lot of valuable time.

• Saturday 23 September •

Your career and professional life are on the up and up, and over the next few weeks you will have to devote large chunks of your time to work-related matters. This could involve quite a juggling act if you are to keep the home fires burning as well. Even though it will be tempting to live up to your Capricorn ability to be a workhorse, try not to slog your guts out when there is no need or when a more relaxed approach will produce better results.

• Sunday 24 September •

Relationships with friends and family are highlighted today and you'll derive enormous pleasure simply from being in their company. Regardless of how strained relations may have been with one particular person recently, you're ready to hold out the olive branch and put an end to any bad feelings. And there's every likelihood that the other person will meet you halfway.

• Monday 25 September •

Are you wondering how to handle a delicate emotional situation? Don't worry, it's not as difficult as you think and is probably more of a storm in a teacup than a full-blown drama. It just requires a little tact and sensitivity on your part to win your loved one over and to dispel the discord between you. If you've both got a sense of humour, you'll soon see the funny side of it.

• Tuesday 26 September •

Don't take anyone at face value today. Someone is trying to smooth-talk you and they may not be completely trustworthy.

Although you're not normally gullible, in this instance you could allow yourself to be manipulated into believing something that has no basis in reality. Use your common sense and don't be fooled by appearances.

• *Wednesday 27 September* •

You're feeling very private today and not in the mood to disclose how you're really feeling. Although you don't want to be rude, you might have to tell someone to mind their own business unless they get the hint. It's not that you've got anything to hide, it's more that you would rather keep yourself to yourself and enjoy your own company.

• *Thursday 28 September* •

Your recent introspective mood has given you the time to think about your current goals and expectations and how far these have progressed. Do you feel that you've had to do a lot of compromising in order to further your ambitions? If so, it might be worth asking yourself if you've adapted yourself too much to what other people want and not given enough consideration to your own needs.

• *Friday 29 September* •

Speak your mind today and say whatever it is that you want to get off your chest. Everything now needs to be out in the open if you're to regain your confidence in the joint aims and aspirations you hold with others. If you have been trusting to luck rather than judgement in a working matter recently, you may find that things get rather dicey over the next few weeks. Try to make sure that you know exactly what you are doing and that you can easily explain your actions.

• *Saturday 30 September* •

Keep a tight hold on your purse strings when you go shopping today, unless you want to end up out of pocket! Not only do you want to spend money on yourself, you're also in the mood to spoil someone special. If they are with you and they happen to have very expensive tastes, let's hope they know when to call a halt! Either way, you will enjoy giving in to your spending urge.

OCTOBER AT A GLANCE

Love	♥ ♥ ♥
Money	£
Career	💻 💻 💻 💻
Health	☼

• *Sunday 1 October* •

It's hard to work out whether you're feeling agitated or you're simply picking up someone else's unspoken anger. In any case, you'll find it quite hard to deal with other people today and your best option is to try to minimize the chance of things getting out of hand. Doing something physical to let off steam will at least mean you're no longer walking around like a bear with a sore head.

• *Monday 2 October* •

Try to find some creative outlet today – even if it's only rearranging the furniture! The important thing is to allow your artistic side to come to the fore and to enjoy expressing it. Even if you doubt that you have any particular talent, you'll be surprised by what you're capable of if you believe in yourself and don't judge yourself too harshly.

• *Tuesday 3 October* •

If you want a quiet life today you would be well advised to steer clear of any subjects connected with politics, sex, religion or anything else that is likely to get steam coming out of certain people's ears. As it is, you could be in danger of having your ears talked off by someone who apparently won't rest until they have browbeaten you into agreeing with every word they say. Why can't they get off their soapbox?

• *Wednesday 4 October* •

You're a force to be reckoned with today, especially when it comes to your work and your public reputation. You're much more likely to make an impact by underplaying your hand rather than by going into overdrive or making your point in a very forcible way. There's a lot to be gained from this strategy, particularly if you're competing for a job or a promotion.

• *Thursday 5 October* •

Although your energy levels are high, you don't have the stamina to sustain them today. The best solution is to pace yourself otherwise you'll be flagging by mid-afternoon, which is just when you need your second wind. It's especially important that you pace yourself if you are well aware of those deadlines that are snapping at your heels. Go carefully and you will meet your targets.

• *Friday 6 October* •

You might find yourself piggy-in-the-middle today and undecided about where your loyalties ultimately lie. You are probably sympathetic to both sides and, unless the decision rests with you, you'd be better off removing yourself from the fray and allowing things to sort themselves out. Your involvement will only cloud the issue and may mean that you are dragged into the argument.

• *Saturday 7 October* •

It's your turn to ask someone to help you with a problem today. Preferably, it should be an older person whom you admire and respect and who is not emotionally involved with you. Capricorns often tend to seek their own counsel, but in this case you are forced to admit that you don't have all the answers and you need to defer to someone's greater wisdom and experience.

• *Sunday 8 October* •

Your perspective is a lot clearer today, which gives you the confidence to make plans. For so long you've been trying to fill in the blanks, but you are now seeing the whole picture and you can steam ahead. Lots of different strands of your life are coming together to make a coherent whole, and anything which doesn't fit into your life will be very obvious.

• *Monday 9 October* •

After yesterday's high, today might seem like a bit of an anti-climax. The reason for this could simply be the release of built-up tension which is making you feel rather tired and depleted. This is only temporary, but you should still take it easy and not put too many demands on your body for a day or two. Once this mood has lifted, it will take wild horses to hold you down!

• *Tuesday 10 October* •

You might have a very therapeutic conversation with someone today that gives you a real boost and fills you with lots of energy. You could talk to someone you're close to, or you might get chatting to a complete stranger that you intuitively feel you can trust. This may seem quite out of character for you but you'll be pleased that it happened.

• *Wednesday 11 October* •

Yesterday's encounter has stimulated your thinking and set off lots of new ideas in your head. This could result in a completely different way of looking at certain aspects of yourself. Perhaps a few of your long-held beliefs are ready to be updated and transformed, paving the way for some new and exciting developments? Watch this space!

• *Thursday 12 October* •

Everyone's eyes are on you today and you're expected to come up with the goods in some way. Take advantage of the fact that you have all the ammunition you need to knock them for six and create exactly the right impression. All you have to do is be yourself and have the courage to say what you think. If you do this, you can't help but make an impact.

• *Friday 13 October* •

If you're a typical Capricorn, you take the opportunity of proving yourself very seriously. You've been feeling even more motivated and ambitious than usual recently and today's no exception. It's a fantastic opportunity to make the right connections and promote yourself in whatever way you can. It's not every day that so many doors are ready to open for you.

• *Saturday 14 October* •

Thank goodness it's Saturday today because with luck you will be able to relax. After the demands of the week, you simply want to switch off and retreat from the world for a couple of days. So what have you got planned? You are in the mood to indulge yourself with lots of delicious food and drink, but try not to overdo it because your system is quite delicate at the moment and could easily be overloaded.

• *Sunday 15 October* •

It's one of those confusing days when your left hand doesn't know what your right hand is doing, and neither does anyone else! You're better off not analysing anything and simply allowing any problems or decisions to float through your head. You might have a gut instinct about what to do or you may feel that you should put things on a back burner until your usual grasp of things returns.

• *Monday 16 October* •

You may still feel slightly disconnected from your everyday life, in spite of the fact that you can function perfectly well. You might prefer to work alone today until you feel like being with people again. If you can't avoid mixing with others, let them know that you're not in the most sociable of moods and, hopefully, they'll understand without taking offence.

• *Tuesday 17 October* •

Look after yourself today because any tense atmosphere will soon affect your health. For instance, you could develop a headache if you have to spend time with someone who always winds you up, or you might feel depressed if you talk to someone who is very gloomy. There is also a chance that you are suppressing anger about something and this is making you feel under the weather or listless. Only you know the answer.

• *Wednesday 18 October* •

It's one of those lovely days when everything goes like clockwork. You can take pleasure in the simplest of activities that you're usually too busy to appreciate. You can also take things that would normally bother you in your stride – they may even give you a good laugh! Whatever is on today's agenda, try to squeeze in something special and which is a bit of a treat.

• *Thursday 19 October* •

Sometimes life more than lives up to expectations and at other times it is full of disappointments. Sadly, this is one of those days when things may not come up to scratch. That is especially likely where your friends and social life are concerned. Something that you were looking forward to could be a non-event or a loved one might be in such a gloomy mood that you wish they would cheer up.

• *Friday 20 October* •

You may have to bite your lip if you want to avoid a row today. On the other hand, things may have reached such a state with a certain person that you think you'll burst if you don't give them a good talking to. If you need to get things off your chest now, make sure you deal with the facts and don't get side-tracked by things that are none of your business or which aren't relevant to the current problem.

• *Saturday 21 October* •

Don't beat about the bush today, otherwise you'll wind up wasting a lot of time and achieving precisely nothing. If you can't get to the point because you're not sure what it is, use someone as a sounding board to help you clarify your thoughts. If not, you'll only spend hours and hours going over things in your head and end up more confused than when you started.

• *Sunday 22 October* •

Act on your hunches today, especially if they concern someone dear to your heart or a romantic issue. You are in a very dreamy and sensitive mood, which could surprise you if you pride yourself on being a practical and down-to-earth Capricorn. You may be like that normally but you certainly aren't today! Relax by listening to music or doing something creative. You will also discover how much a certain person means to you.

• Monday 23 October •

Give yourself plenty of elbow room today to manoeuvre yourself through a potential minefield. It's hard to know who you can trust and who to be wary of, and you'll need to keep all your wits about you. There's very little information to go on, but as long as you rely on your instincts and a gut sense of timing, you'll come up trumps.

• Tuesday 24 October •

Whoever thinks they have the upper hand over you is about to discover that they've badly underestimated you. What transpires between you and a work-related person could mark a turning point in the way you deal with others, especially if you are able to stand up for yourself. If you remain firm but flexible, you really have nothing to fear.

• Wednesday 25 October •

Go out and have fun today, especially if it's with someone you have a very close rapport with. You're able to make the people you're with feel very good about themselves and you take real delight in one another's company. This is a tonic for you both and gives you the breathing space you need from all those recent ups and downs.

• Thursday 26 October •

Proceed with extreme caution today, especially when tackling anything connected with finances or possessions. A certain person may not be as honest as you imagine, or they may have a hidden agenda that won't do you any favours at all.

Although this is no reason to become paranoid, you should still look after your own best interests but make sure you remain honest, open and trustworthy.

• Friday 27 October •

Life hasn't always been a bed of roses this month but what happens today will help to make up for all that. Something could make you forget all about a current worry or you might realize that you have been stewing over nothing. There could be good news about a health matter or a colleague could do you the sort of favour that will earn them a place in heaven.

• Saturday 28 October •

A certain person could easily seduce you into changing your mind today, and you need to determine what the effect of that might be. It may only be inconsequential, but on the other hand it could be disastrous. Try to stay impartial and weigh things up carefully. If you can't trust yourself to remain objective, wait until you can judge the situation more clearly even though this person may be piling on the pressure.

• Sunday 29 October •

You're all set to take the initiative and get the ball rolling today. All forms of communication are looking good now and you'll be doing your fair share of both listening and talking. You're able to create a receptive and friendly atmosphere so that everyone can be heard and get their point of view across. This bodes well for a successful outcome.

• Monday 30 October •

Your popularity is on the rise today, and you could hear from lots more people than usual. Friends could ring you up or you might receive several social invitations that have you leafing through your diary trying to juggle dates. It's a fabulous day for any form of group activity because your customary shyness will disappear and you will feel happy to talk to whoever happens to be around, even if they are a complete stranger. They won't stay that way for long!

• *Tuesday 31 October* •

Everything runs smoothly today and you're able to reap the rewards for your past efforts. Give yourself the credit you're due and, although you probably won't spend too long resting on your laurels, enjoy this space of relative calm. If you're a typical Capricorn, you'll soon be thinking about what you can do next.

NOVEMBER AT A GLANCE

Love	♥ ♥ ♥
Money	£
Career	💻 💻
Health	☼ ☼

• *Wednesday 1 November* •

It's almost as though you've got a layer of skin missing today, because you feel much more sensitive than usual. You may take something to heart that wasn't meant as an unkindness but that you nevertheless feel wounded by. You would normally be able to laugh it off but, because you're feeling so vulnerable, you feel more like bursting into tears. Call a good friend to the rescue!

• *Thursday 2 November* •

Your emotions are still just beneath the surface although you feel as though they're about to spill over any second. If you feel a strong need to talk about how you're feeling, make sure you confide in someone you can totally trust and who's sympathetic to what you are going through. The last thing you want to do is make things worse by getting the cold shoulder.

• *Friday 3 November* •

However much you try to settle down and relax, the pace of events around you is so busy that you eventually get caught up in it. There's no point in trying to think things through until the tempo slows down again and allows you to keep your mind in one place. When that happens, you'll be able to collect yourself and get back into balance. In the meantime, go with the flow!

• *Saturday 4 November* •

Capricorns often prefer to be their own boss and the coming seven weeks are a particularly good time to aim for some measure of autonomy and independence. You have everything to play for now, and you are also feeling extremely ambitious! So decide what you want to achieve and then set your sights firmly on that objective. You will feel very single-minded about this, and full of determination to succeed.

• *Sunday 5 November* •

Someone's nose could be put out of joint today, and if so you might be the culprit. You're so preoccupied with your own projects at the moment that you may be neglecting your nearest and dearest. However, they aren't going to let you get away with it, and they may make their feelings very clear on the subject. If you end up in everyone's bad books, all you can do is try to repair the damage and eat a little humble pie.

• *Monday 6 November* •

You can kiss goodbye to any thoughts of being in control today! There are forces at work that threaten to totally disrupt your routine. These might be someone who won't stop talking or circumstances beyond your control. Your first reaction is probably panic as you frantically attempt to get on top of things. A more effective strategy might be to stop dead in your tracks, evaluate the problem and then decide how best to remedy it.

• *Tuesday 7 November* •

A lot is expected of you today and you'll need to pull out all the stops in order to fulfil all those high hopes. Although you have always been more than willing to help in the past, you may now be starting to resent the fact that your partner or business associate assumes that you'll always bail them out in a crisis. This might be a good time to say how you really feel.

• *Wednesday 8 November* •

Communication difficulties have blighted the past couple of days, leading to frayed tempers and a lot of time-wasting confusion. You may have been running round in circles after someone who can't get organized or someone might have led you on a wild goose chase. Thank goodness everything is now returning to normal, giving you the chance to repair the damage and then concentrate on more important matters. Phew!

• *Thursday 9 November* •

You believe in your ability to succeed today and you are willing to take certain risks so you can prove yourself. If you are involved in a pursuit that offers you the opportunity to grow in new ways, you'll fight tooth and nail to make the most of it. Other people may not share your enthusiasm or your drive, but this is a quest that has tremendous meaning for you and you won't be deterred from following it.

• *Friday 10 November* •

Material security is very important to most Capricorns. You know that money is necessary to achieving your goals, and you also know that you only feel truly safe when there is money in the bank. So this is a great day for devising a money-making scheme that will put you on a stronger financial footing. If this involves selling your talents and your ideas, you're on to a winning formula!

• *Saturday 11 November* •

You may have to make some necessary adjustments to your social life over the next two weeks. For instance, if you are already making your plans for the festive season, you may have to rethink some of the arrangements. It's a marvellous time to begin your Christmas shopping because you are in the mood to seek out lovely gifts for your nearest and dearest. You might even fancy making some with your own fair hands.

• *Sunday 12 November* •

If your self-confidence is flagging you can count on a certain person to help restore it today. In fact, this person will be more helpful than you realize, and you should pay attention to any suggestions they have to offer because you'll benefit enormously from them. If you have ever doubted their loyalty to you, you will now realize that you have done them a disservice. They are completely on your side after all!

• *Monday 13 November* •

Dust off your party clothes because you are going to need them during the next few weeks! Your popularity starts to rise by leaps and bounds from today, and you will be in great demand socially between now and early December. You will also be even more charming than usual, and a certain person will have stars in their eyes whenever they look at you. So prepare to be worshipped and adored – somehow, you will manage to get used to it!

• *Tuesday 14 November* •

It's a wonderful day for partnerships, and you will find it easy to get along with whoever happens to be around. If you usually pride yourself on keeping a stiff upper lip, don't be surprised if someone or something manages to get past your defence mechanisms and touch you deeply. It might be something that seems quite insignificant to everyone else but which gets your bottom lip quivering.

• *Wednesday 15 November* •

Your passions are ignited with a vengeance today and it might be hard to keep a lid on them. How much you allow yourself to express these intense emotions to a certain someone could be the source of much inner turmoil. If your greatest fear is that your advances might be rejected by this person, you may decide to wait until you're absolutely sure that your feelings will be reciprocated.

• *Thursday 16 November* •

You're being given a leg up the career ladder today and it's important that you don't fall into the trap of exaggerating your abilities in the mistaken belief that you'll make a better impression that way. Have faith in yourself and you'll come across in exactly the right way and, provided you don't assume that you already have all the answers, everything will fall into place.

• *Friday 17 November* •

You have a lot to be thankful for today because there are plenty of opportunities to improve the quality of your relationships and your life in general. You're able to reach a new level of understanding that makes you feel much happier and more secure in yourself. A friend could be a real pillar of strength or you might admire the way they stand by you through thick and thin.

• *Saturday 18 November* •

Being a Capricorn, you probably have a fairly strong code of ethics that guides you in your life. If you're faced with a decision today that puts this code to the test, make sure that the way you behave is beyond reproach and that no one will be able to accuse you of stepping out of line or doing the wrong thing. If in doubt, err on the side of caution.

• *Sunday 19 November* •

You are now in a position to show how strong and capable you really are, and you won't have any problems in winning approval. You are only too happy to volunteer your services and do more than your fair share if necessary. Your willingness to help with whatever is needed simply to get the job done is the best investment you can make to win deserved appreciation for all your hard work.

• *Monday 20 November* •

You reach some sort of pinnacle today and someone will be singing your praises. If you usually play down your accomplishments, you'll probably find all the fuss somewhat embarrassing. Your cheeks may turn redder than Rudolph's nose! If, however, you tend to take great pride in your achievements, make sure you capitalize on all the acknowledgement that you receive now. It'll give your ego a massive boost.

• *Tuesday 21 November* •

You can coast along today and not feel that you have to justify every minute of the day. Your self-worth is often determined by your effectiveness but today you can just feel good about yourself without having to do anything in particular. And if you get the opportunity to go out and have fun, make sure that you squeeze every drop of enjoyment out of it that you can!

• *Wednesday 22 November* •

You might well be the only dissenting voice in what turns out to be quite a heated debate today. If you are at loggerheads with everyone else and you feel strongly about defending your position, use your intuition to find the best way to resolve the disagreement. You'll come up with a much more imaginative solution than any amount of logic or reason could provide.

• *Thursday 23 November* •

Be wary of anyone who promises you the earth today because, despite their good intentions, it's unlikely that they will come up with the goods. It's much better to say no to what they propose, rather than to pretend that you are going along with their ideas out of sheer politeness. It will be far wiser to be straight with them, because if you aren't you may have to do a lot of back-tracking later on.

• *Friday 24 November* •

You have many assets that you can draw on when you need to and quite a few of them are on full view today. This gives you the chance to make a conquest that has eluded you until now. Knowing how appreciated you are gives you the incentive to extend yourself into areas that you didn't dare previously venture into. So be brave and be prepared to push back another boundary and step out into the world.

• Saturday 25 November •

If there is a difficult atmosphere or raised voices today, it will be very tempting to try to act as the peacemaker. However, rather than pacify someone it may be better to say exactly what you think. This could require courage on your part, especially if the person concerned is jumping up and down in a rage, but do you honestly have a choice? Try not to make matters worse by mixing business and pleasure unless it is absolutely necessary.

• Sunday 26 November •

In contrast to yesterday's courageous mood, you're more of a soft touch today and you can be sure that someone is ready to take advantage of the fact. This time, however, you are more than happy to indulge them because you know that their motives are completely above board. For instance, you might give your time or money to a charity or good cause. In any event, the pleasure you get from giving will make it all worthwhile.

• Monday 27 November •

It's one of those days when you need to keep on the move, otherwise you will quickly start to feel bored, stale or fed up. You may also wish to give a wide berth to anyone who is apparently living in the dark ages or who refuses to move with the times. Take note of any bright ideas that come to you because some of them could be real crackers, especially if they are connected with your finances or your hopes for the future.

• Tuesday 28 November •

Keeping your personal and professional lives separate could be a very difficult task today. The problem is that colleagues and associates are feeling intensely curious about you and they might ask some searching questions. You may not want to divulge anything at all because you are feeling quite private at the moment. Perhaps the best solution is to make light of the whole situation and try to change the subject.

• *Wednesday 29 November* •

It will be easy to speak in the heat of the moment today and then wish you hadn't. For instance, you could be direct to the point of being blunt with someone at work and run the risk of alienating them. This is especially likely if they happen to be in authority over you. Even if you have little respect for this person, you should choose your words carefully.

• *Thursday 30 November* •

You're feeling quite sentimental today and you might even get out the old photo albums and take a nostalgic wander down memory lane. This is an ideal time to reminisce with old friends about times gone by and to enjoy a good laugh about some of your most embarrassing moments. You'll feel as though you've had a holiday without moving from your front room.

DECEMBER AT A GLANCE

Love	♥ ♥ ♥ ♥ ♥
Money	£ $ £
Career	💻 💻 💻
Health	☼ ☼ ☼ ☼

• *Friday 1 December* •

New people are coming into your orbit today and one person in particular could become a very good friend. You share a lot of common interests and, as you get to know each other better, you will realize how similar your goals and aspirations are. Don't be surprised if this person ends up playing a very important part in your life in ways that you can't possibly imagine at this stage.

• Saturday 2 December •

There's an inexplicable air of excitement around today that you can't help absorbing. It will either make you feel slightly edgy and restless or it will give your energy levels such a massive boost that you go into overdrive. Either way, you're probably not the most relaxing person to be around right now, and if you notice everyone giving you funny looks, you'll know why!

• Sunday 3 December •

You don't want to be hemmed in or pinned down today, and you need to find a way of burning off all that excess energy. If you're the physical type, a brisk walk or a jog round the block would be a wonderful idea. If that doesn't appeal, you really need to find another sort of activity that will tax your brain or challenge you in some way. If not, you'll end up climbing the walls!

• Monday 4 December •

You are totally engrossed in whatever you do today and, because you're so focused, you will be able to achieve an enormous amount. It's important that you're selective in what you actually decide to concentrate on, otherwise you may end up spending hours on something that is relatively unimportant. Your best bet is to tackle the things that are top of your list of priorities first and then work your way down.

• *Tuesday 5 December* •

Family obligations are high on the agenda today and you might be asked to sort out a difficult problem that can't be ignored any longer. Whether this is easy or tough will depend largely on your ability to understand all the complexities of the situation. It might be a good idea to think everything through before taking action. By the way, you may have to use a large amount of tact!

• *Wednesday 6 December* •

You're ready to break through a big barrier today that has prevented you from doing something that you didn't think was possible. Once you have achieved this successfully you will realize that the main hurdle was convincing yourself that you could do it. This will come as a big vote of self-confidence, because you will know that you have a lot more strength and guts than you gave yourself credit for in the past.

• *Thursday 7 December* •

A financial opportunity could materialize over the next few weeks that will make a significant difference to your bank balance. In fact, money will be so easy to come by that you will probably immediately want to spend some of it! A good way to invest the money will be to buy something that you will treasure and which will increase in value. That way, you can be extravagant without feeling guilty.

• *Friday 8 December* •

If you have to learn something new now, you'll catch on so fast that it will take you hardly any time at all to be on top of the situation. Your boredom threshold is very low today, so the more there is to learn and the more challenging it is, the better you will feel. Anything that doesn't stretch you won't be able to keep your attention for very long. You need to be inspired.

• *Saturday 9 December* •

This is a wonderfully romantic day when something that you've been fantasizing about might actually come true. If so, you will be dancing on cloud nine! On a more mundane note, there could also be some great news about a work or health matter. You may feel that your guardian angel is looking out for you or that everything has fallen into place at the right moment.

• *Sunday 10 December* •

It's another day when you feel glad to be alive, and when life offers you many blessings. If you are going to a festive party, you will want to eat, drink and be merry. You will have a whale of a time! If you are currently on a diet or some other form of health regime, you may abandon it briefly when you are faced with too much temptation. Go on, live a little!

• *Monday 11 December* •

Being of service to other people will give you a lot of satisfaction during the coming fortnight. This might involve looking after someone who is suffering from the seasonal sniffles, or it could mean helping someone get all their Christmas preparations out of the way. You might also do some serious thinking about your job prospects, especially if you want to make a lot of progress in 2001 but you first need to clear the decks in some way.

• *Tuesday 12 December* •

If problem-solving is something you relish, you'll be in your element today. That is especially likely if the difficulty has stumped other people who normally pride themselves on getting to the bottom of things. It is also a good day for solving a mystery that has perplexed you recently, but try to avoid letting it dominate your day to such an extent that you end up being unable to think about anything else.

• *Wednesday 13 December* •

You expect to get as much out of life as you are prepared to put into it today. You can cope with almost anything and you can push yourself to the limit without wearing yourself out. No one has higher expectations of you than you do yourself, and your competitive streak is encouraging you to be the best in whatever you tackle. However, don't be too hard on anyone who is struggling to keep pace with you.

• *Thursday 14 December* •

You aren't feeling as fired up as you did yesterday, and as a result you're more willing to make concessions and compromises. If you have been in someone's bad books recently, now is the time to swallow your pride and patch things up. If your apology isn't accepted straightaway, don't see this as a reason to become defensive and back off. Be patient and give it time.

• *Friday 15 December* •

Are you starting to worry about all the Christmas preparations that are still outstanding? If you don't know which presents to buy for certain people, a brainstorming session today will be very productive. You could have some very bright ideas. Alternatively, you might decide to stroll around the shops and wait for inspiration to strike.

• *Saturday 16 December* •

If you have had a busy week, the last thing you want to do today is slog your guts out. However, before you can start to enjoy yourself there may be one or two chores to get out of the way. A certain person may try to persuade you to give them a hand with something, but you have other fish to fry. Today is a good opportunity to organize some forthcoming travel arrangements, such as buying your tickets in advance to save time on the day.

• Sunday 17 December •

The compassionate side of your nature is very apparent today and you may feel drawn to help someone in need or to give some money to a worthy cause. You want to make a difference and you'll extend yourself in whichever way is available to you. By the same token, whatever help you need now will almost certainly arrive, provided you remember to ask. It really is that simple!

• Monday 18 December •

It's one of those days when you are determined to get a lot done, especially if you have certain deadlines to meet before you can start your Christmas holidays. Draw up a list of what needs to be tackled first, and then get cracking. You may find that you are better off working under your own steam than following someone else's orders, although you are quite happy to be part of a team if that is your only option.

• Tuesday 19 December •

A few question marks could be raised in your mind today about a financial matter or a private problem. Be prepared to think things through carefully and, if necessary, to confide in someone who will be able to give you some good feedback. You might discover that you have a secret admirer when they drop hints or make suggestions. Are you pleased about this or do you want to run a mile?

• *Wednesday 20 December* •

If you often find it difficult to be around certain people because they have such an uncanny knack of rubbing you up the wrong way, you can heave a sigh of relief today. Instead of feeling irritated by them, you are perfectly willing to humour them and to make allowances for them. As a result, your relationship will be much easier and a lot more productive. This will be especially useful if the person in question is your boss or an older relative.

• *Thursday 21 December* •

Stand by for some good news! You start to come into your own today, and over the next four weeks you will be blessed with a lot more confidence and energy than you have felt recently. This is the ideal time to forge ahead on personal projects and plans, because they stand a good chance of getting off the ground. So decide what you want to achieve over the next twelve months and then go for it.

• *Friday 22 December* •

This is a good day to put across your point of view without getting anyone's back up. You will be able to choose your words carefully, especially if you feel very strongly about something. However, try to marshal your thoughts before talking about anything very important, otherwise you might jump from one idea to the next in such a way that everyone wonders what on earth you are talking about. If you can make a conscious effort to slow down, you will be extremely effective in making some important points.

• *Saturday 23 December* •

The next few weeks will be a really productive time if you can get on well with others. However, if there are too many differences of opinion, nothing will get done. You might even end up falling out with each other. Be prepared to be the one who has to take responsibility for sorting everything out and making sure that everyone is happy.

• Sunday 24 December •

There are some big surprises in store today, and these may not be very welcome if you are frantically trying to do a million things at once in readiness for tomorrow's celebrations. If you are passing the shops, you could spot something that you simply must have, no matter what it says on the price tag. You might also be taken aback when you realize for the first time how much someone or something means to you. It's as though you never noticed it before.

• Monday 25 December •

Happy Christmas! And what a wonderful day it is going to be, especially if you can be with some of your favourite people. You will love chatting to whoever happens to be around, and you might even spend ages on the phone talking to friends and family who live far away. It's one of those days when you feel ultra-sociable, and you will happily join in with all the fun and games.

• Tuesday 26 December •

Even though you may still be in the thick of the festivities today, it's a good time to start thinking about any changes that you want to make to your life. You are feeling so up-beat and confident that you are prepared to entertain ideas and objectives that would usually seem too ambitious or far-fetched. However, over the next two weeks you will be willing to give them your best shot. They could lead to the birth of a brand-new you!

• *Wednesday 27 December* •

If you are afraid that your emotions are running away with you and you're desperately trying to get them under control, don't fall into the trap of pretending that you don't feel anything at all. Capricorns often pride themselves on being cool, calm and collected, and they can feel very out of sorts when they're not. If this applies to you, compose yourself by all means but give your feelings room to breathe.

• *Thursday 28 December* •

Are you feeling hot under the collar? If so, you'd be far better letting off steam now than allowing an upset or annoyance to build up and reach boiling point. You'll be amazed how quickly everything blows over once you've said your piece. In any case, you'll be only too happy to put the whole thing behind you and restore the peace with everyone concerned.

• *Friday 29 December* •

Go carefully today because you could easily feel hurt or disappointed by what happens. Someone might make a chance remark that cuts you to the quick or deflates your ego, but did they really mean to hurt you? Unfortunately, a social event may turn out to be a bit of a non-starter, or the person you hoped to meet there may be conspicuous by their absence. Try not to get too upset by what happens now.

• *Saturday 30 December* •

Thank heavens you are starting to feel happier today. There will even be times when your energy knows no bounds. This is an ideal day to start something that you've been putting off for a while, because you now have the enthusiasm to get things moving. However, unless you feel excited about this particular project you still won't get it off the ground! Anything that feels remotely like a chore won't hold your attention for five minutes.

• *Sunday 31 December* •

If you have been gearing yourself up for New Year's Eve over the past few days, no one is going to enjoy tonight more than you. Whether you opt for a big party or a small gathering, you're going to have a great time. And whatever your goals and aspirations are for 2001, you certainly won't be thinking about any New Year resolutions until you've recovered from tonight's excesses! Have fun!